The American Dream

Chevrolet Impala

1958-1970

Veloce

www.veloce.co.uk

First published in November 2019, reprinted Ocober 2022 and February 2023 by Veloce Publishing Limited, Veloce House, Parkway Farm Business Park, Middle Farm Way, Poundbury, Dorchester DT1 3AR, England. Tel +44 (0)1305 260068 / Fax 01305 250479 / e-mail info@veloce.co.uk / web www.veloce.co.uk or www.velocebooks.com. ISBN: 978-1-787113-10-7; UPC: 6-36847-01310-3.

Contents

Preface

In this, our 15th motoring book, my son and photographer Andrew Mort and I have once again combined his photographic talents with my knowledge, research and writing to tell the fascinating story of the evolution of the early generations of America's one-time dream car: the iconic Chevrolet Impala.

Andrew personally handled all the images, advertisements and brochures – scanning, enhancing, cropping, recording, filing, and packaging – as well as accompanying me on trips shooting and collecting information.

Much appreciation for some excellent additional photography goes to Carol Duckworth, Jason Brant, and Media Relations super gal, Christine Giovingo of Mecum Auctions; Grant Cairns of Cairns Automotive Sales Literature; the Petersen Museum, and the extremely helpful Heather Buchanan of Kahn Media, Inc (who shared the Impala images from its *The High Art of Riding Low: Ranflas, Corazón e Inspiración* exhibit that featured the celebrated Chicana/o artists and their rolling sculptures); Legendary Motorcar Company (LMC); Country Classic Cars and the many other Impala enthusiasts whose cars are featured in these pages.

At this time, Andrew and I would also like to thank Rod Grainger, Tim Nevinson and the knowledgeable and dedicated team at Veloce Publishing for their highly professional publishing skills, continued encouragement and faith in our historic vehicle books.

It should be noted that upon researching our books I discovered annual production totals varied considerably, as well as for various models and bodystyles. Some were perhaps due to simple human error, while others were educated estimates, or figures sourced from the factory at different times.

Often the published production totals were provided for the calendar year, while others were for the model year; sometimes these were sales figures, other times they were production figures, and this was not always clarified. Some sources simply based the total on previous findings. Other reasons for discrepancies in totals may be due to including Canadian production and, sometimes, export figures. I hope I am not perpetuating errors, and, whenever possible, I have used the Automobile Manufacturers Association (AMA) as a source.

Owning a brand new Chevrolet Impala in the late 1950s and throughout the '60s was once the American Dream. The late American President Woodrow Wilson wrote, "We grow great by dreams. All big men are dreamers. They see things in the soft haze of a spring day or in the red fire of a long winter's evening. Some of us let these great dreams die, but others nourish and protect them; nurse them through bad days till they bring them to the sunshine and light which comes always to those who sincerely hope that their dreams will come true." Thank goodness for the Impala enthusiasts who followed their dreams for all of us to still enjoy.

Introduction

It doesn't get much better than a bright red 1958 Chevrolet Impala convertible. This Impala was a 'dream car' back in 1958, and it's a dream car to own and drive to car shows today. Like many past GM cars, the Impala started out as an additional trim line to an existing model, featuring upgraded performance, added chrome, some distinctive badges, and a deluxe interior.

The Chevrolet Impala was an image maker in the latter half of the 1950s for Chevrolet, and General Motors as a whole.

In 1950 Chevrolet filed for the copyright of the jingle *See The USA In Your Chevrolet*, which was soon heard all over North America. In fact, the jingle went on to become synonymous with famous singers such as Dinah Shore and, later, Pat Boone. Although *See The USA In Your Chevrolet* was sung by many others over the years, one of the most memorable renditions was the raspy crooning of the Los Angeles Dodgers' radio and television broadcaster Don Drysdale.

That (combined with the stirring television introductions of the newest Chevrolets during the 1960s by famed Canadian war hero, actor, and broadcaster Joel Aldred, and actor and announcer Lorne Greene – particularly known as a headlining star on television's *Bonanza*) pushed the Chevrolet nameplate into the living rooms of America. So popular was *Bonanza* on a Sunday night that it introduced Americans to Chevrolet's newest line-up for years.

Thus, it wasn't surprising that, almost overnight, the Chevrolet Impala became the dream car for many Americans.

From an industry standpoint, as the 1950s came to a close, the Chevrolet Impala was going to play a major, albeit somewhat subtle, role in the increasingly popular 'personal car' market.

The stylish Chevrolet Impala had quickly caught the imagination of America's emerging upper middle class, and, as the popularity of the Impala increased, the model evolved and took on the status of American icon.

The Impala also became the prestige family model proudly parked in thousands of new suburban driveways all around the country. While not everybody could afford an Oldsmobile, Buick, or, especially, Cadillac, by the later half of the 1960s, GM could offer you a Cadillac clone in its luxurious and powerful Chevrolet Impala.

The Impala was soon a status symbol, and Chevrolet added more and more style, comfort and optional equipment to the ever-increasing model range over the years.

While the Impala models of the late 1950s and

early '60s were the flashy, stylish, colorful, two-tone, and often most powerful siblings in the Chevrolet line-up, it would ultimately return to a more conservative, high volume, mainstream car by the end of the next decade.

This book examines the evolution of the popular Chevrolet Impala from the stylish, specialty vehicle of the late 1950s, to Chevrolet's best-selling, most iconic model in North America during the 1960s.

The Impala's wide range of specifications and bodystyles, rarer performance models, and optional equipment are examined, and specific industry facts and figures pertaining to the Impala line-up are also included.

This is all accomplished through detailed text, references to contemporary road test reports, brochures, period factory and advertising images, along with previously unpublished photographs to relive the American Dream of owning a Chevrolet Impala.

Although a comprehensive book in many areas on all things Impala, not every fact, figure, etc could be included due to space. However, we have attempted to include more than enough information to satisfy the keen Chevrolet and Impala enthusiast.

The Chevrolet Impala became an American icon and dream car. Over the years, many of the models in many of the bodystyles appealed to Americans of all ages. Some loved the styling flair, others the luxury and ride, but for many it was the handling and performance of the big Chevy. In that performance category, the 409 was near the top! This one graced the cover of *Car Life Magazine* (3/63).

The postwar era and constructing the road to the American dream car

By the end of the Second World War, North Americans desperately needed new cars and trucks. Automobile production had halted by 1940 in Canada, and early 1942 in the United States.

In 1945, the Automobile Manufacturers Association estimated that 48 per cent of the cars in America were at least seven years old.

While the war-torn populace and manufacturers in Europe and Britain faced the reality of bombed factories, a crucial loss of skilled labor and huge material shortages, the North American automobile manufacturers were quick to convert factories back to full-scale vehicle production. Ford emerged first to build new cars starting on July 3, 1945.

The pent-up demand was a boon to the industry. America's independent automobile manufacturers, such as Hudson, Studebaker, Kaiser-Fraser, etc, were quick to market fresh designs, while the traditional Big Three were slower off the mark with all-new models. However, Ford, General Motors, and Chrysler had a better parts supply and distribution system, a strong dealer network, and production volume on their side.

Soon new production facilities were springing up all across North America. Chevrolet had opened new passenger car and truck assembly plants in Flint, Michigan and Van Nuys, California by 1947.

In 1949 the automotive industry broke a 20-year record by producing an all-time high of 6,235,651 units.

Yet, by the mid-1950s the remaining independents were all struggling for survival as General Motors, Ford, and Chrysler cut prices, continually introduced new models, fresh styling, and the latest in innovations and modern mechanicals. America's involvement in the Korean War had certain negative effects, but the Big Three were much more immune than the remaining smaller, already struggling, independent automakers.

At the same time, the Big Three were competing head-to-head, attempting to become the leader in America's automotive market, with an eye to becoming the dominant car and truck builder worldwide.

On the American domestic scene, it was, once again, Ford versus Chevrolet for top dog.

Prior to 1955, Chevrolet, as General Motors' most affordable automobiles division, tended to follow the architect Louis Henry Sullivan's (1856-1924) aphorism: "form follows function." Although hardly bland, the Chevrolet Division focused on building solid, practical, reliable transportation with little in the way of pizazz.

Ford had introduced its new 239ci OHV V8 in 1954 and Chevrolet returned the volley with its small block 265ci V8, which signaled the start of the horsepower race.

Soon multi-carbs, fuel-injection, and superchargers were available from the OEM or from a prolific aftermarket.

Chevrolet stepped-up its racing image in NASCAR, while its Corvette began to make a name for itself in sports car racing. Chevrolet's performance image was emerging steadily by the mid-1950s.

The battle for sales leadership had gone on for years. Despite the fact that Ford had originally outsold all its rivals, including Chevrolet, in the first decades of the 20th century, Chevrolet had topped Ford in popularity and sales by 1929.

Over the next ten years, the sales leadership between Ford and Chevrolet changed back and forth, and, by the mid-1950s, new cars and model trim levels appeared annually.

Chevrolet tended to dominate, but knew Ford was more than capable of capturing the number one sales position in any given year.

The V8 and lesser six-cylinder engines continually grew in size and power. Although there were a few economic downturns, sales increased steadily and the demand for bigger and better became an American passion.

Financial credit became easier and easier to secure, gasoline was cheap, and times were good.

In 1956 Chevrolet unveiled a Corvette concept car dubbed the 'Impala' as a stylish hardtop.

In 1955, Chevrolet began pushing performance through its many advertisements in American enthusiast magazines. The accompanying text bragged about its many triumphs in America's highly publicized NASCAR races. "Chevrolet's got it! Enough high-powered punch to run the pants off competition, all competition, including most of the so-called 'hot high-priced cars!'"

The name and styling cues proved popular with the car show-going public. As a result, the idea was soon translated into a new model, developed by Chevy chief engineer Ed Cole, and studio designer Jerry Cumbus.

In fact, the complete redesign of the full-size, A-body Chevrolet began mid-year, 1955.

Bigger and better was the theme as the marketplace boom was in medium-priced cars. Prosperity and the demand for more luxury, comfort, and performance was obvious in car, and even pickup truck, sales.

As the design of the '58 models progressed, there was an interest in creating a more exclusive 'Bel Air Executive Coupe,' which would ultimately become known as the Impala.

For much of the population in the late 1950s a house in the suburbs, some money in the bank, and a flashy new automobile in the driveway was the modern American dream.

Ultimately, the full-size Chevrolet Impala would become, for many, one of the elements in this idyllic future.

By 1957, automotive stylists were spreading chrome over an automobile's sheet metal as generously as peanut butter on a kid's sandwich. Throw in pastel, two- and three-tone colors, powerful V8 engines, wide whitewall tires, and tail fins, and American cars sparkled after years of economic hardship, war, and the ongoing threat of a 'Red Invasion' or nuclear mushroom clouds. American car buyers loved it. Chevrolet's new, ritzy California 'Bel Air' image was about to take another giant leap ahead with the introduction of the high-style Impala in 1958.

Impala – the magic in a name

The Bel Air Impala had lots going for it in style, comfort, and power, yet designers created even more allure and excitement in its chic badging, insignia, and script. The crossed flags would become an instantly recognizable Impala crest, as would the graceful chrome image of a leaping impala. The Impala emblem was perhaps inspired by Jaguar's leaping feline. And, while an impala was a graceful and fast running antelope that inhabited the African plains far from North America, it was a superlative symbol. Instantly recognizable, Ford would later employ its own animal artistry and inspiration on the Mustang, Cougar, and Pinto.

There was a lot more to the new, finless, fresh-looking, full-size 1958 Chevrolet Impala model than met the eye. In fact, it was all new!

In 1958, Chevrolet introduced a girder chassis as the foundation for a lower, wider, and longer body. The chassis featured standard full-coil spring suspension on a 2.5in longer, 117.5in wheelbase.

Designed by Ed Cole and Harry Barr, the all-welded, 'Safety Girder,' X-type frame also reduced the overall height without sacrificing headroom, and was 30 per cent stronger than the previous frame.

Other notable new mechanical features included anti-dive braking and a foot-operated parking brake.

Styling-wise, the front end treatment, while reminiscent of past models, now highlighted more intricate, sculptural design.

The 1958 Chevrolets also featured dual headlamps for the first time, and virtually abandoned any signs of a fin by instead adopting a unique concave contour in the rear fenders which accentuated the highly sculptured look.

The new Impala model was only available as a coupe or a convertible. The convertible was the only one in the Chevy line-up. Both the open and hardtop (Sport Coupe) models were top-of-the-line to the already up-market Bel Air 1800 Series.

The two rear sets of triple taillights immediately identified the high style, high-priced Impala.

The fashionable, but 200-300lb heavier, Impala also sported all the trim features of the lesser models, plus Impala script, insignia, and checkered flags emblems; ribbed stainless steel rocker panel covers; imitation rear fender scoops ahead of the rear wheel wells, along with other added trim; a competition boomerang-shape, two-spoke, deep-dish steering wheel; and a rear seatback, with a built-in, centered radio speaker grille.

As a major sub-series of the Bel Air model, the new $2693US Impala Sport Coupe and $2841 base price convertible had to be easily recognizable as the ultimate Chevrolet models. In 1958 there was a full range of more powerful engines available when you ordered your Impala. For those looking for glamour on somewhat of a budget, you could even order the base 235.5ci inline six. Proportionally few were delivered because, for a few dollars more, the healthy V8 was a very attractive option. Four powerful versions of the 283ci V8 and three versions of the 348ci V8 were offered.

All in all, from the A-pillar back, the Impalas differed substantially from the rest of the full-size Chevrolet line-up. The Impala Sport Coupe also featured a shallower greenhouse and longer rear deck, along with its distinctive roof/body two-toning.

From a marketing point of view, Chevrolet moved out of the low-priced field with the Impala, and into the mid-price range traditionally covered by Pontiac and Oldsmobile.

The Impala could also be viewed as Chevy's new

While the new top-of-the-line 1958 Bel Air Impala came fully loaded, many '50s buyers were quick to add popular dealer options and custom aftermarket accessories. Although not the biggest V8, the 283ci engine with fuel-injection was considered the hot motor by many. The Corvette fuelies were equipped with the 283ci V8, as were the some of the Chevrolet NASCAR entries in its dominating 22 wins. Yet, the 348ci V8 would eventually evolve into the legendary 409. In '58 the 280hp, 348ci V8 was capable of propelling the 3669lb Impala from 0-60mph in just over nine seconds, and record a ¼-mile run between 16-17 seconds at nearly 85mph.

entry into the emerging 'personal car' field to offset the spotlight and glamour of Ford's bigger, newly-unveiled, four-seater Thunderbird released in '58, as well as the all-new Edsel. The Impala advertising of the day focused on style, luxury, performance, and handling.

In its '58 brochures, Chevrolet immodestly proclaimed that the new Impalas were "Excitement on Wheels."

A standard 145hp, 235.5ci 'Blue Flame' six was offered, or you could opt for the, now standard, bigger 185hp, 230hp, or fuel-injected 250hp 283ci 'Turbo Fire'

V8, as well as two other versions. Optional too, was the truck-sourced 'Turbo Thrust' 348ci V8 engine, offered in three different power levels rated from 250-315hp. Power was transmitted via a two-speed automatic transmission or three-speed manual depending on the horsepower ordered.

In June 1958, the American car magazine *Motor Life*, took an in-depth look at all the V8 engines that were currently offered. While horsepower numbers were omitted and speed downplayed, the American car manufacturer didn't detune its 300hp engines, reduce bore and stroke, or halt engine development. This was regardless of the fact that, in 1957, the AMA had established a new policy on horsepower and speed in advertising.

Chevrolet not only tricked out its small block, but introduced the 348ci V8, and, according to *Motor Life* magazine, "Right now the 283ci engine appears to develop a true output of over 80 per cent of rated power (say 190hp from the standard 230hp power pack), while the big 348-incher averages less than 75 per cent (or maybe 180-190hp for the 250-rating). Neither engine is very good on fuel economy in relation to car size and weight."

Meanwhile, *Sports Cars Illustrated* (1/59), pointed out that one could order the 348ci 'Law Enforcement' engine capable of 0-60mph in 7.2seconds and a 96mph, 15.2second ¼-mile.

And, as for old Chevy six, *Motor Trend* magazine (7/58) compared the six-cylinder Chevrolet to the V8 and found that the six returned somewhat better fuel mileage figures, but a substantially slower (by six seconds) 0-60mph time.

The tester's conclusion was, "To me, it [the six], would be worth nothing. I would rather buy a little more gasoline and enjoy modern transportation. I don't believe there is a person in this country who would like to live in a cave just to save the rent or mortgage payments on the house he is living in."

The all-new 1958 full-size Chevrolet line-up had lots going for it. The Chevy was far more than just new sheet metal, and the Division was eager to educate buyers on its many modern features. Yet, while there were numerous new safety and mechanical improvements, Chevrolet focused on imprinting on customers' minds its exciting, top-of-the-line, more exclusive Impala model in the handsome Bel Air series. The Impala Sport Coupe's B-pillar was borrowed directly from the Corvette show car of the same name. The side trim and wrap-around grille motif was also inspired by the 1956 Corvette concept.

While all the 1958 Chevrolets were built on a wheelbase of 117.5in with an overall length, up 9in, to 209.1in, technically, the Bel Air Impala Sport Coupe and convertible differed in height at 56.5in and 56.4in respectively. This was lower than the standard Chevrolet models by an inch. Both the convertible and Sport Coupe measured in at a width of 77.7in. The creases in the Sport Coupe's roof and rear air vent were apparently inspired by the Mercedes-Benz Gull-Wing. The sizeable dimensions also provided plenty of interior room, including generous hip and legroom in the rear seat.

The Impala interior was created by Ed Donaldson, Chief of the Chevrolet Interior Studio. And, back in 1958, it was the dressiest and most comfortable of all the Chevrolets. A choice of colorful materials and patterns, nylon carpeting throughout, and lots of chrome were in fashion. The seat upholstery was tricolored, and the door panels were color-keyed with showy brushed aluminum inserts. The color-matched, painted dashboard also featured added aluminum trim and the distinctive Impala script. A unique two-tone, two-spoke, deep hub sport steering wheel was standard. The clock was a popular optional extra.

In 1958, with gas selling at around 20 cents per gallon in America, nobody really cared.

Motor Trend (1/58), ran a comparison test between the 280hp, 348ci V8 Impala Sport Coupe; the 305hp, 350ci V8 Plymouth Belvedere two-door hardtop; and the 300hp, 352ci V8 Ford Fairlane hardtop.

Ingress and egress to the Impala scored the worst of the three, but all three of the two-door coupes were criticized concerning the difficulty in getting into the rear seat.

The Impala dash layout was declared as having far superior ergonomics: "It is a relief to find an instrument panel well laid out for the driver's convenience."

In 1958 the flashy new Impala was competing in the Ford Thunderbird, high-end Ford Edsel, and larger, flashier Chrysler and DeSoto market. And while the T-Bird is credited with creating the niche 'personal car' market, the slightly larger Chevrolet Impala was just as glamorous and powerful, and provided better value. The body panels were unique to the Impala. The doors, decklid and rear fender extensions were not interchangeable with Chevrolet's Bel Air, Biscayne, or Del Ray models. Although the styling of all the 1958 Chevrolets is considered typical over-the-top 1950s, to many eyes it is the look of the Impala that has best withstood the test of time.

Equally praised as superior was the Impala's comfort, driving position, and visibility; it was also acknowledged as always being easy to start compared to the competition.

As the report noted, "The steering column is almost horizontal and the wheel position is of the arms-almost-straight-forward type that inspires confidence in the driver. The seat is firm, comfortable, and adjustable ..."

Driving around town, the Chevy was harder to park, having no power steering, but upping tire pressures from 26lb to 32lb transformed the Impala into "... a cross-town ride that was once the exclusive property of chauffeur-driven, gray-haired ladies."

On the highway the Impala scored top marks, with *MT* testers noting, "... very little body roll. Road noise is of a very low level." And, on rough roads, the Impala's new suspension layout was also highly commended.

The Turboglide two-speed automatic transmission was an update of the Powerglide. It was never the best, but graded by most road testers of the day as passable.

The stopping power of the Impala's non-power, four-wheel drum brakes lacked the grip of the new disc brakes that were beginning to appear throughout the industry, but were considered more than adequate, nevertheless.

MT concluded "The Impala should easily win acceptance from the sports-minded automobile enthusiast. It's a solid car, with good cornering characteristics, plenty of power, and a chassis that should hold up under a rugged life."

While most American makes saw sales slip by about 30 per cent in a recessionary 1958, Chevrolet was number one in sales with over 1.2 million, compared to Ford's sales figure of fewer than one million units.

In fact, the all-new full-size Chevrolet – aided by its instantly popular Impala models, (a total of 181,469 of which 55,989 convertibles and 125,480 Sport Coupes or 15 per cent), helped the GM Division capture an incredible 29.5 per cent of the total US car market.

The Impala was clearly a big hit!

Opposite: Two options introduced by Chevrolet were the 'Level Air' suspension (1958-1957) and the Turboglide automatic transmission (1957-1961). Both added unnecessary expense, and both proved troublesome due to being rushed into production for competitive reasons. The $124US optional Level Air suspension offered little benefit over the new standard suspension, and the Turboglide, although smoother, was unreliable, difficult to repair, and expensive to fix. As well, these options were not popular and thus disappeared after just a few years.

While a red 1958 Impala was a real attention getter, an arctic white convertible with a red and silver interior, was an equally classy ride. In addition to all the standard sparkle, it was especially true when all the popular iconic dealer options and aftermarket accessories were fitted, such as a Continental kit, rear fender skirts, dual rear fender mounted aerials, wide whitewall tires and more were added. The rear seats of an Impala came standard with a fold-down armrest and an integrated radio speaker. *Motor Trend* magazine (1/58) declared it "the car to capture those interested in an American Gran Turismo."

The 1959 & 1960 batwing Impalas

In 1959, Chevrolet advertising boasted that "Chevy's Got a Car That Leads Your Kind of Life" and, looking at this Impala, many buyers would have loved to have had that kind of life. With all-new body styling, all-new frame, a longer 119in wheelbase, and another 2in longer in overall length, the new full-size Chevrolet was now the longest car in its price range (in 1957 it had been the shortest). On the outside, the Impala was 5in wider than in '58, and the interior 3in wider. The Del Ray line was dropped, and the Impala Series became the top-of-the line with a full range of models. (Courtesy LMC)

NOTHING'S NEW LIKE CHEVY'S NEW!

Proclaiming 'Body by Fisher' was still a big selling point in 1959 as far as General Motors was concerned, yet to most buyers by then, it was just a nice emblem always placed on the threshold plate when the door was opened. In 1959 the Impala line-up included the two-door Sport Coupe, a convertible, and had added a four-door hardtop and sedan. There was no two-door sedan or station wagon Impala. Chevrolet called its rear batwing shape a "saucy rear deck." Although industry distinctive, the 'cat's eyes' rear lights were not an embraced design feature and were gone in 1960.

Despite the fact that the full-size Chevrolet was all-new in 1958, the 1959 was totally different. As a separate series now, the new top-of-the-line Impala also included a four-door hardtop and sedan. (Chrysler made a similar move making the Fury its new high-priced Plymouth, and demoting the Belvedere in status.)

As a cost-cutting exercise, Chevrolet would share the same unit construction bodyshell with Pontiac, Oldsmobile, and Buick in 1959. All four cars would feature unique styling, but share the majority of the engineering design and mechanical features cloaked from the view of the buyer.

In 1959 the full-size Chevrolets bore the expansive, batwing rear fender and trunk styling. The fins were horizontal, which led famed auto tester Tom McCahill to declare there was, "... enough room to land a Piper Cub."

Longer, lower, wider, and roomier also came with extensive changes to the chassis, suspension, and

The 3580lb 1959 Sport Coupe (two-door hardtop), was sleek and modern, with many interesting styling cues, such as its practical, though 'jet age'-looking, vent design over the rear window. The Impala Sport Coupe had a basic price of $2717US, and a production run of 157,100 out of the 473,000 Impalas sold in 1959. The gas filler cap was now hidden behind the rear licence plate. E-Z-Eye tinted rear glass was a popular option in the sunshine states. About the only thing the 1958 and '59 Chevys had in common was the wide side trim in a contrasting color.

engines. Although reduced 1in in overall height, the headroom actually increased by 1.5in.

An enhanced rear suspension helped offset the size and weight increases, while also improving the handling and reducing sway. Larger brake areas with better cooling aided stopping, and the optional Turboglide transmission was improved. The standard 3-speed shift could be had with optional overdrive ($108.00US). The Corvette four-speed was also optional.

There was a choice of eight different V8s, plus the new, de-tuned six. The most powerful was, at first, the 315hp, 348ci, but later a 320hp, and 335hp would appear; in total there were six other power levels offered in '59! Still, hot rodders loved the fuel-injected 283ci V8.

Overall V8 performance was up slightly, as were the rather dismal fuel economy numbers.

The 10hp less six improved economy by 10 per cent, lesser so on the upgraded V8s.

The longer 119in wheelbase was standard on all four, full-size series and wouldn't increase again until 1971.

A four-door hardtop and sedan were added to the new top-of-the-line Impala model range, while the two-door hardtop and convertible remained exclusive to the Impala.

Motor Trend (1/59) noted, "Driving ease has been improved by relocating the front seat and steering wheel for better visibility. A 74 per cent increase in rear glass area makes for easier parking and maneuvering in heavy traffic." And, although the steering was lighter, it was still described as a "bit slow."

Sports Cars Illustrated magazine (7/59) tested a lesser Chevrolet Bel Air sedan with just the $44.15US chassis options added. It was dubbed, "A Family Man's Corvette," by accomplishing a 0-60mph time of 8.4 seconds with a ¼-mile run accomplished in 16.7-seconds at 94mph.

The W-348 powered Chevy had fallen under the direction of famed Zora Arkus-Duntov, who credited General Manager Ed Cole with the improvements in handling. In an interview Duntov openly stated Cole was interested as much in driving as he was in making cars.

Motor Trend (12/58) discovered that the Chevrolet '59 'Police Pursuit,' with a 3.36 rear axle ratio, could top 135mph.

The Impala nameplate had made a big splash in its first year and Chevrolet was determined to ensure that marketplace excitement would continue in 1959, especially with all the enthusiasm generated in the press and in the showrooms.

So, when Ford management first viewed the dramatically restyled Chevrolets, they figured the warmed over '59 Fords would be dead-in-the-water.

However, the new, dramatically different, Harley Earl-directed Chevys were not as well received as expected. A distinctive appearance, as Ford had learned with the Edsel, was just too different for Americans to accept.

Ford model year sales were not a disaster, although Chevrolet did top Ford. The difference was less than 20,000 and that was including Corvette sales. Chevrolet's production total for the model year was 1,481,070 versus Ford's 1,462,140 units.

However, due to a strike that affected GM, Ford easily beat Chevrolet in overall calendar sales in 1959.

In 1960 the Impala's wings were clipped somewhat by designer Clare MacKickan, and that toned-down the rear end styling. The teardrop rear lights and matching front end styling chrome eyebrow air intakes also gave way. Up front a rounded chrome-laden trim was added to an overall cleaner grille.

The front end styling had been left to Bob Cadaret who convinced GM and Ed Cole of Chevrolet, to push for the more oval-shaped look. Both designers worked together on the side treatment, and were influenced by the new jet aircraft with vapor trails.

While the $2662US six and $2769US V8 1960 Impala four-door hardtops had lots of panache, they were also highly practical, and could carry six adults in snug comfort with their front and rear bench seats. Chevrolet touted its 'Custom Comfort' ride, which, according to the brochures, saw "... a husky coil spring at each wheel to soak up road shock and vibration before it reaches passengers." Other sources of additional comfort included new, larger body mounts, 'scientifically' applied sound deadening insulation, a longer wheelbase, and a wider track.

While the rear end styling was the subject of countless discussions throughout the car world, the full-size Chevy's front end treatment was also unique. The Impala sported the same grille and high narrow nostrils as the other full-size Chevrolet models in '59, but added atop the Impala fender crowns were rocket wing trim for an even flashier, jet-like appearance.

Not too many young, red-blooded, American men could resist getting behind the wheel of a race-winning stock car. In 1960 Chevrolet's competition department and sales teams were firm believers of the 'win on Sunday, sell on Monday' philosophy. The Impala was the model that could offer it all – from performance, comfort, and luxury, to a high-flying image of success.

The 1960 Impala was the Chevrolet Division's model in the evolving 'personal car' niche market. While its competition often aimed its sights on the American male college graduate, up-and-coming young executives, or older, more distinguished, businessmen, Chevrolet also realized many women would be buying and driving its Impala. Still, in this era before the next wave of the women's rights movement, the typical-of-the-time, chauvinistic male advertising people perceived most of those female buyers as suburban housewives and moms who were self-absorbed, overly fashion conscious, and wanting to be seen in the latest trendy, brightly colored, and high styled car.

SPACE

SPIRIT

SPLENDOR

'60!

CHEVROLET!

With the four non-functional, lower rear window molding air-intakes, and its contrasting white spear on the rear fenders, the Impala was still not subtle in styling, but far less outrageous than the '59 versions.

The rooflines remained the same except for the lower placing of the air extractor on the Sport Coupe. The optional full-wheel discs were also less gaudy.

The 1960 Impalas remained large cars at 210.8in and could still be ordered with the base 135hp, 235.5ci Six, or the optional 283ci V8 at 170hp (de-tuned by 15hp in quest of better fuel economy!).

Other choices included a 4bbl carb at 230hp, or the 348ci V8 engine at 250-335hp, depending on option preferences.

Once again, the three or four-speed manual transmission was available, or the automatic Powerglide or Turboglide transmission.

Some substantial chassis changes for 1960 included additional frame bracing, a reworked driveshaft tunnel, improved braking, optional power steering, and a new parking brake design.

Inside there were different vinyl and cloth materials and colors, but these were just as showy as in '59.

The dash was little-changed other than an all-new sport steering wheel design.

Additional options consisted of a more basic four-way power seat, cruise control, rear window defogger, and a trunk release. Two once-popular '30s, '40s, and '50s options were dropped: the continental rear tire carrier and cowl mounted spotlights.

The advertising copy of the day proclaimed the 1960 Impala embodied, "Space – Spirit – Splendor."

The top of the-line, heavily chromed 1960 Impalas found over 411,000 buyers. And that was despite the six week strike that limited availability in the last quarter of 1959! The full-size 1960 Chevy outsold the equivalent Ford models by almost half a million units.

The 1960 Impala 3625lb Sport Coupe (two-door hardtop) at $2704US was not as expensive as the top-of-the-line convertible ($2945US), but was equally desirable, especially painted in Jade Green. Although not the most popular color today, green would become the 'fave' color in North America by the end of the decade. Many were ordered powered by Chevrolet's 348ci V8 fitted with the 4bbl carburettor.

The airy-look of the Impala four-door Sport Sedan (hardtop) – seen here in Roman Red – provided excellent all around vision, but could get quite warm on hot, sunny days. The unusual wrap-around rear windscreen was unique to the four-door hardtop model, and added plenty of

style. A total of 411,000 Impala models were built in 1960, of which 169,016 were Sport Sedans. Standard equipment on all 1962 Impala models included sunvisors, electric wipers, a cigarette lighter, front armrests, foam seat cushioning, a parking brake, glove compartment, backup lights, anodized aluminum trim, an electric clock, and oil filters on all V8s.

The least expensive and best-selling model added to the 1960 Chevrolet Impala line-up was the four-door sedan. This two-tone example was sold in Tasco Turquoise and Ermine White. Chevrolet felt even the four-door sedan was a, "… tasteful blending of Impala beauty and sedan comfort." A full-size Chevrolet station wagon was available in the lesser Bel Air and Biscayne trim models, but not in the top-of-the line Impala series

The most expensive Impala model was the convertible. The 1960 Impala Convertible was described in its brochure as being the, "… newest version of America's most fashionable convertible." Chevrolet offered a choice of four vinyl convertible top colors: white, black, red and blue.

In 1959, Chevrolet built 72,265 Impala convertibles, nearly 18,000 more than in 1958. The 1960 Impala convertibles sold even better, with that number rising to 79,903 ragtops. Although flashy, the 1960 Impala convertibles, like the rest of the line-up, sported far more muted colors than those offered in 1959, although red and white can never be considered subtle. (Jason Brant, photographer, courtesy Mecum Auctions)

New sleek & slim 1961 and 1962 dream Impalas

1961 was a big year for Chevrolet! As the most prolific GM Division, Chevrolet built its 44 millionth vehicle.

In addition, it also marked the end of a classic styling era under the direction of Harley Earl, who had retired in 1958. The 1961 Chevrolets ushered in an era of less exuberant flamboyance, replaced by a more functional, yet still fashionably styled design, under the direction of William Mitchell.

As a result, 1961 was a big year for the high flying Impala too!

The full-size Chevys sported a new, stylish, fresher '60s era look. The once-popular tailfins of the past decade were gone for good on Chevrolets.

Motor Trend (11/60) described the new rear end styling as, "incorporating a gentler and refreshing rounded appearance."

The customary banks of Impala rear end tri-lights were individual and incorporated into flush units, but with bullet lenses and embellished aluminum bezels.

The front end styling was reminiscent of the previous year, but the A-posts were thinner.

The fender and door treatment was cleaner and less rounded for an overall trimmer appearance.

Whereas some of the styling cues of the 1959 and '60 full-size Chevrolets had been outlandish, the 1961 models could be described as handsome and svelte. There were no gimmicky, contrived, look-at-me, styling prompts.

Full-size Chevrolets were seen as hot cars in the showrooms and on the track. Racing not only improved the breed, that helped establish a winning image. Pictured is a 1961 Chevrolet, piloted by famed racer Louis Unser, winning that year's Pikes Peak Auto Hillclimb for stock cars. Unser and Chevrolet also shattered the old 1957 record by shaving off more than half a minute to set the new mark at 15.06 minutes. Yet, when you talk about performance, it was the soon-to-become-legendary 409ci V8 that Chevrolet would be most remembered for in 1961.

Opposite top: The 1961 Chevrolet Impala four-door hardtop Sport Sedan was deemed a handsome and sporty looking, yet a very practical, family automobile. The hardtop fulfilled all the needs of a growing family with spacious and comfortable accommodation, while providing a cavernous trunk to haul all that necessary cargo required on long journeys. The Sport Sedan was also the perfect busy executive and businessman's car, great for transporting clients and any sizeable work-related items in style.

Opposite bottom: The 1961 Impala models were described in brochures as being a "Trim New Size" with "Clean New Style," and "Fine New Comfort." The four-door hardtop Sport Sedan now featured a far more conventional C-pillar and rear window design. This example was painted in Jewel Blue.

CHEVROLET FOR 1961

The 1961 Impala was more spacious inside with increased legroom and fitted with higher back, more erect seats. Egress and ingress were also improved with wider doors and lower door sills. The foam cushioned seats included new rich fabrics in six brighter, fresher colors and patterns found only on the Impala. And, the Impala interior came with an electric clock, a parking brake warning light, longer armrests, and deep-twist carpeting throughout as standard. The Chevy models also came with a lower console. Note the driver enjoying the oh-so-popular at the time, stereoscope View-Master, which first appeared at the New York World Fair in 1939 – and is still in production today.

Like all the big Chevrolet models, the Impala featured a generous trunk. The lower trunk sill (apparently, as much as 10.5in lower than some competitive models), allowed for the loading and unloading of bigger, heavier and bulkier items far more easily. A deeper trunk also permitted taller items to be hauled in a closed trunk. Although the spare tire was neatly stored out of the way on the higher back shelf, it meant unloading a great deal of the cargo if you had to take it out during these days of more-commonly-occurring tire punctures. The 14in tire and steel rim was also heavy and cumbersome to remove.

While the drivetrain and mechanicals were generally the same, the suspension had undergone more extensive revisions to improve the Impala's ride, comfort, and handling. All the linkage was now rubber-bushed, the front and rear coil springs with tubular shocks rested on rubber pads, lower trailing arms were added on each side to control drive and torque while maintaining axle alignment, and an upper control arm was fitted, as well as a lateral bar to control sway. Anti-dive and vibration improvements also provided a safer and quieter ride.

1961 was also the year the sporting pretensions ended for the Impala and this full-size, handsome, luxury image car got serious about performance with the introduction of the Super Sport or 'SS' models. Those chromed initials emblazoned on the sheet metal instantly translated into "beware of the performance machine."

You could personalize any of the five Impala models to the SS level. There were the usual glitzy, show-off options such as a padded instrument panel, a front passenger grab handle, 8.00X14 narrow whitewall tires, and simulated knock-off, full-wheel disc covers, but some of the serious stuff included a steering column-mounted Sun 7000rpm tachometer, beefier springs and shocks, and metallic brake linings.

The Impala Sport Coupe was not only stylish, but, due to its narrow roof pillars, provided the best all-round vision of all the models offered. The narrow-front-to-wide-rear side slash trim in a contrasting white paint with chrome, emblems, insignias, and script were unique to the Impala line-up, as were the chrome fender top wings.

From the rear, all 1961 Impalas were immediately recognizable by the full-width upper rear chrome trim and the double set of triple taillights. Unlike the bright trim seen on the 1960 Impala models, the tail panel was again painted in matching body color. This Impala four-door sedan was factory sprayed in Sateen Silver, which, unlike today, was not a popular color in 1961.

Like all Impalas, this four-door Sport Sedan in Arbor Green was equipped with deluxe, full-wheel discs and wide whitewall tires. Back in 1961, the 3570lb Sport Sedan had a dealer sticker price of $2769US.

Under the hood, SS owners could choose one of three versions of the 348ci V8, offered from 305hp to 350hp.

The least powerful V8 could be mated with the 2-speed Powerglide automatic transmission, while more V8 power could be handled by an optional four-on-the-floor stick shift.

Neat stuff, but only 453 Impalas were sold in 1961 with the 'SS' option and most were Sport Coupes.

Yet, the biggest event of 1961 for the power hungry Chevy lovers was the mid-year unveiling of the 409ci V8.

While the 265ci V8 and its evolving variants had transformed Chevrolet's stoic, but reliable persona back in the '50s, it would be the 409 that brought Chevy to the performance forefront in the 'Swinging Sixties.'

And while the big 348ci V8 had never really shed its sober truck heritage with enthusiasts, the bigger, brawnier sourced 409ci V8 became an immediate superstar engine. Almost overnight, the 409 instantly and rightfully became the proclaimed king of performance on the streets and dragstrips across North America.

Just 142 of the 360hp, 409ci V8, 0-60mph in seven seconds, Super Sport versions were sold in 1961.

One was purchased by Dan Gurney who entered his off-the line, nearly stock 409 at Riverside and broke the lap record by a full second. Then, in the British Saloon Car Championship race at Silverstone competing against the likes of Hill, Parks, and Salvadori in Jaguars, he led the entire race until a wheel came off just two laps from the checkered flag.

The 1961 Impala Convertible was even more of a fashion statement than the sexy Sport models. It was Chevrolet's heaviest and most expensive model in the line-up. Weighing in at 3600lb and costing $2847US, around 64,600 were delivered to happy buyers in 1961 out of a total Impala production of 491,000 units.

New for 1961 in the Impala series was a two-door sedan starting at $2546. It featured a new, squared-off 'canopy roof' with narrower C-pillar styling and a wrap-around rear screen. Its upright design provided a very different look compared to the slender, sloping rear pillar of the two-door Sport Coupe. This two-door sedan was painted in the unusual Coronna Cream.

This dual purpose, dual appeal 1961 Chevrolet advertisement also featured a play on words with "The Greatest Show on Worth." In today's world an ad like this would be immediately rejected. The base Biscayne four-door sedan was promoted for its practicality and economy, while the Impala Sport Coupe shown was, "... one of five luxury-loving Impalas." What American wouldn't want to aspire to own an Impala and have that pictured lifestyle?

For 1962 the full-size Chevrolets were further decluttered and lost even more curves.

Added this year were the six-passenger ($3068US) and nine-passenger versions ($3171US) of the Impala Station Wagon. After climbing onto the fold-down tailgate, the third seat passengers faced rearward.

The two-door sedan was removed from the Impala line-up.

The highly popular and distinctive Impala two-door hardtop was restyled with a more formal and substantial wide C-pillar.

The *Motor Trend* magazine (7/62) report stated,

"The Impala's hardtop styling brought general approval. Simple and to the point, it is one of the cleanest, best thought-out designs to come along."

MT road tested the Sport Coupe or hardtop to answer the question, "What puts the Impala at the top of the popularity poll?"

Luxury was high on the list, as well as the now traditional long list of Impala attributes. The $2776US base price soared to $3275US with the addition of the most popular optional equipment, which included the 170hp, 283ci V8; power steering and brakes; a Powerglide transmission; radio; and whitewall tires.

While the full-size 1962 Chevrolets appeared to not be radically different in styling, the fender treatments and front and rear end revamp resulted in a completely fresh look. In reality, though, all the sheet metal was new except the door panels. The wheelbase remained unchanged at 119in, but the overall length was stretched slightly to 209.6in. The headlamp treatment was simplified, the full-length side slash became more like a belt line, and the rear end regained its shiny sparkle. The changes were all cosmetic, with the major components and mechanicals remaining basically identical to 1961.

In 1962 the Impala interiors underwent a few minor changes. As well as featuring all the Bel Air upgrades, there were a host of standard Impala fittings. The Impala interiors had always been plusher and upgraded. The vinyl materials appeared to be richer thanks to a leather grain look, and the polished aluminum and chrome-like trimmings on the seats, door panels, armrests, dash, and steering wheel added an appreciated period classy, glitter. And, regarding trunk space, *Motor Trend* magazine (7/62) declared, "There is just one whale of a lot of room available."

After a few days of testing, the scribes wished they had opted for the **SS** package which included the more comfortable individual bucket seats.

The 283ci V8 was praised for its flexibility and more than adequate performance, with a top speed that approached 100mph and a 0-60mph time of under 13 seconds. Optional was the 'new for '62,' 250hp or 300hp 327ci V8, for those wanting more oomph. Then again, for mind-blowing acceleration, the 380hp or 409hp, 409ci V8 could be ordered.

While comfort, a quiet ride, and smooth highway cruising were in the Impala's favour, its handling in fast corners, ride on rougher surfaces, and hard braking weren't.

As *Motor Trend* pointed out in its report, "A few manufacturers try for a compromise between suspension soft enough for a comfortable ride, yet firm enough to offer good, safe cornering ability but Chevrolet prefers good ride."

And, as for brakes, the "Power brakes require very light pedal pressure and it is impossible to make hard stops without locking up all four wheels." (In Chevrolet's defence, all American power brakes were overly sensitive – or felt that way – in the '60s. Drivers, after years of slamming their feet down on American cars' hydraulic brakes, found it difficult to adjust. And alas, disc brakes were still a rarity on most American cars of this era.)

Other criticisms included derogatory comments about the over-sized steering wheel, which didn't help the already excessively slow steering; a perceived sloppy linkage; the excessive body lean; and front end plowing. *Motor Trend* still concluded, "The Impala with the standard V8 fills the bill – a solid sensible car with a dash of luxury."

At the 1962 Winternational Drag Races, the top stock car at the meet was a 409-powered '62 Chevrolet that was prepared and driven by famed Don Nicholson. His winning quarter-mile run was recorded at 12.62 seconds, at 110.95mph. Note the front wide whitewall tires. *Motor Trend* (7/62) stated, "If you're looking for a good base for winning 'Super-Super/Stock' at the drag strip, this is a good bet. Or if you just want a big car with brutal road performance, this will fill the bill." Everyone seemed to be singing the Beach Boys popular song *409*: "Giddy-up, giddy-up, giddy-up, 4-0-9 ..." With a 0-60mph time of 6.3 seconds, Chevrolet and performance were synonymous.

Impala Convertible buyers had a choice of colors for their folding vinyl tops. While many opted for a strong, contrasting black, white was popular for a white-on-white effect that, in many ways, provided a more harmonious flair. A white vinyl top also accentuated the now-popular narrow whitewalls. The convertible tops were power operated, but not lined or padded inside. A snap-on vinyl boot cover hid the metal framework and unfinished looking vinyl underside to provide a cleaner, smoother look for top-down cruising.

Many described the 1962 Impala's styling as less pretty, and more bold and purposeful. Fewer curves and an angular, sculptured look was the evolving trend. It would also be the last year for the bent windscreen A-pillar. The straight contrasting color slash, body crease line, and polished rocker cover rocketed your eye to an almost arrowhead front fender tip. This new styling made the just two-year-old 1960 Chevys look prehistoric in comparison. The squared-off styling was a hint of what to expect of the all-new Chevrolet Impala evolving in 1963.

Bigger dreams, higher performance – 1963-1964 Chevrolet Impala

Any hints of the sleek looks of the 1961-62 Impalas were gone in '63. The Impala was even more angular, boxy, and upright in design, yet the wheelbase remained the same. The extensive face-lift and completely reworked bodyside contours provided a fresh new look. The Sport Coupe was offered with an optional vinyl roof for '63. Overall, the styling of the new Impalas was designed to appear like a more expensive luxury car. The buyers loved it. A total of 832,600 Impalas were built in 1963 of which 735,900 were powered by a V8 and 153,271 were Super Sports.

Impala station wagon sales reached 198,500, with 146,200 being equipped with V8s. The example pictured is a nine-passenger (three-seat) wagon in Laurel Green. Available only as a four-door, the Impala Station Wagon was also available in six-passenger form. With the seats folded a voluminous 97.5ft³ was available. For easier loading, the lift-over of the fold-down tailgate was only 30.6in high, while the opening was 30.5in high and 56.5in wide. The tailgate was counter-balanced with a power rear window, which was optional on the six-passenger and standard on the nine-passenger wagon. One advantage of the two-seat wagon was a concealed, rear 10.5ft³ storage area in the floor.

The Impala model line-up was unchanged in 1963, and the Super Sport series was still offered only in Sport Coupe and convertible form.

Canada Track & Traffic (6/63) opened its 1963 Impala Super Sport road test by posing a question and then answering it: "Are the days of the big, hairy American automobiles in the Duesenberg, Packard tradition really gone? Not so, if the Chevrolet Impala Super Sport is any indication. With no lack of reverence for the great classics of the past, we'd say our test car has all the power, plushness and performance, comparatively, of the denizens of three decades ago. Only the fact that it uses stock bodywork prevents it from having a potentially classic distinction." (That point has now changed.)

Although the full-size Chevrolets were not totally new in appearance, the final vestiges of curves and sweeping spears were gone. Yet, the Impala was seen by most as embodying both style and practicality.

CT&T (6/63) magazine described the Sport Coupe in these terms: "Styling is pleasantly simple, featured by a creased roof intended to resemble the lines of a convertible ... the designers have done a good job of making it look fleet and sleek."

When it tested the Impala SS 409, *Car Life* (3/63) pointed out that high horsepower wasn't the only thing to consider, "... the engine in our test car develops more torque than the 425hp model over the speed range most used, ie from 500 to about 3500rpm. Stated another way, the high torque 409/340hp engine's advantage extends

One of the most popular bodystyles in 1963 was the handsome two-door hardtop, or, in Chevy's lingo, the Sport Coupe. Prices started at $2774US for a base V8 version, but, if you were to opt for the Super Sport sub-series, the bottom line was $2913US with lots of options still to choose for increasing your motoring pleasure. The 409ci V8 engine options gave buyers a choice of 340hp at 5000rpm, 400hp at 5800rpm, or 425hp at 6000rpm. This was possibly Chevrolet's personal 1960s interpretation of the often heard cultural protest, "Power to the People!" (Jason Brant, photographer, courtesy Mecum Auctions)

The Super Sport interior was advertised as having "real sports car style." As well as being roomy, comfortable, and elegant, it exhibited all-vinyl front bucket seats framed in aluminum trim, and an aluminum-topped full console housed the sport shifter along with a lockable stowage compartment. There was a choice of either the Powerglide automatic or a four-speed, all synchromesh transmission. A color-keyed exterior/interior color combination was offered. The seven interior material colors consisted of fawn, aqua, red, blue, green, antique saddle, and black.

from 10 to 80mph and at any speed in-between it will have more high-gear punch than the 409/425hp engine."

Car Life also noted that although the 409ci V8 wasn't as smooth as the 283ci and 327ci V8s "... the difference is barely noticeable. Fuel consumption is a little heavier ..."

All the magazines of the day recommended adding the heavy-duty springs and shocks, and the metallic brake linings to any Impala. And, testers of the day still complained about the steering, driving position, cornering, front end plowing, and the inevitable brake fade.

The interior of the 1963 Impala was, once again, quite distinctive. As usual, the Impala was equipped with all the features found in the Bel Air series, plus such added delights as patterned upholstery and a grained, leather-like finish to its vinyl surfaces, added polished aluminum side seat trim, foam seat cushions, matching tufted vinyl door panels with different armrests, a sport steering wheel, a clock, and extra warning lights, courtesy lights, and supplementary trim.

Still, *Car Life* concluded, "... while we criticize some of the minor things about the car, we can enthuse over its general concept. Big and strong, with a smooth transmission and plenty of muscular draft horses up front, it begins to approach the ultimate in US performance cars."

And, in an earlier *Canada Track & Traffic* Car Council Awards issue (1/63) the magazine chose the full-size Chevrolet for many practical reasons, but focused on the ease of service, parts availability, reliability with little attention, and engineering.

From the rear, the aluminum panel and twin set of triple taillights continued to immediately convey the message that you were behind an Impala. Other telltale features included the distinctive Impala insignias, script, front fender trim, added wide stainless side spear trim and dressier, full wheel discs. The faithful, aging base 283ci V8 featured a power increase to 195hp. The 250hp or 300hp, 327ci V8 engine with the Powerglide automatic transmission were the most commonly ordered options. (Jason Brant, photographer, courtesy Mecum Auctions)

The 1963 Impala Series was the only full-size line to offer a four-door hardtop Sport Sedan. With a sticker price of $2839US, the Sport Sedan was a large, handsome model with generous room and comfort for up to six passengers. Its stretched rear deck provided a trunk capable of holding liberal amounts of luggage and personal items. Like all the full-size Chevrolet and Impala models, it was built on a 119in wheelbase with an enormous overall length of 210.4in.

The Chevrolet Impala dream now included all those Americans who put practicality and reliability ahead of luxury, performance and style. The times were changing and so was the Impala.

By 1964 Ford and Chevrolet owned over 50 per cent of the American automobile market. And, of course, Chevrolet was just one Division of General Motors. In the full-size car market, Ford – with its Custom, Galaxie, and Galaxie 500 – captured 11.5% of the market selling 845,292 cars; Chevrolet with its Biscayne, Bel Air, and Impala line claimed 21.7%, building 1,593,245 automobiles.

The least expensive Impala model offered was the four-door sedan, which sold in the largest numbers. The single man who had owned an Impala in 1958 now needed the convenience of two extra doors for his young family. Businessmen also appreciated the generous rear seating for clientele. In contrast, this '63 brochure illustration shows the less practical, but very sporty, convertible. Whereas 561,511 four-door sedans were assembled, only 82,659 convertibles rolled off the line.

Those figures were about to change dramatically with Ford's introduction of its sensational new 'Pony Car,' the Mustang. Here was a new American star that – although less practical – was an instant image maker.

When combined with Ford's "Total Performance" marketing push, growing popularity of the mid-size Ford Fairlane, and the blue oval's success in both North American racing and on the international scene, Chevrolet was about to suffer a minor setback.

If that wasn't enough, the Impala in 1964 was also about to come up against some sales threatening competition within its own division and parent company.

Whereas the compact Corvair and Chevy II had been no threat, the addition of its own intermediate-size sibling, the Chevelle (and the other new slightly smaller GM models), would be.

Automotive scribes over the previous few years had relentlessly criticised the Impala's overall size as unnecessary. And then there's the logic of 'why buy a Chevy when you can have just a slightly smaller, fully equipped, more prestigious Pontiac, Buick, or Oldsmobile?'

These models were all, indirectly, serious sales competition, but in some market demographics they were direct challengers.

Styling changes were minor, with the most notable being squared-off fender corners and a more sculptured look overall. 1964 Impala production totalled 73,600 six-cylinder cars, a whopping 616,000 powered by V8s, and an additional 185,523 SS models. (Note: Impala station wagons were not included in the totals.) Once again, the Impala Series was immediately differentiated from its lesser Biscayne and Bel Air siblings by its flashy full-length side trim, taillights, badging, etc. Thundering Super Sport identifiers included SS emblems, SS wheel discs, additional trim bits and an 'turned aluminum'-style dash and side trim inserts, bucket seats, plus all the Impala features.

The rear end styling in '64 was subtly changed, with the largest section of the rear panel returning to body color, and the aluminum trim reduced to provide an eyebrow effect. Added chrome trim pieces ran through the centres of both the front hood and trunk lid. The trunk, thanks to a lengthy overhang, was huge, leading *Canada Track & Traffic* (6/63) to state "We've seen pickup trucks that don't have as much room. Perhaps someone will offer conversions to make it suitable for sleeping or carrying the family dog."

Opposite: Before the Chevrolet 350 became the engine of choice over the following decades, the 327ci motor (1962-69), was the enthusiast's favourite V8. The Turbo Fire with the 4bbl carb and dual exhaust was rated at 250hp, but that could be upped to 300hp or even higher to 340hp. The legendary, all powerful 400 to 425hp, 409ci V8 was a less practical engine, but was popular as the crowned king of the stoplight drag races and a choice of 8684 keen, power hungry Chevy enthusiasts in 1964.

Car & Driver (1/64) compared the full-size Ford and Chevrolet models, and noted the dramatic change in marketing.

"There are many options available. This is one of the most significant developments in American automotive merchandising in the last six to eight years. The factories can take one basic body, chassis and engine and offer you various 'packages' all the way from a luxury town carriage to an out-and-out racing car."

The Impala 409 was also facing new competition. Inside the GM camp, Pontiac unleashed the hot GTO, while Oldsmobile introduced its 4-4-2.

Ford was equally outfitted with powerful V8s. Customers could order a full range of V8s, with the topper being the 427ci rated at 425hp with dual 4bbl carbs. The 427ci V8 was also offered in lesser 410hp and 400hp levels.

Meanwhile, in '64, Chrysler unveiled its rubber-burning 426ci 'Hemi' engine on the NASCAR circuit.

The '64 Impala and SS Series were the only full-size models available as a handsome two-door hardtop. The Sport Coupe (Model 1847) had a starting price of $2786US. For a mere $175US you could order your Sport Coupe in Super Sport guise. The Super Sport models were now a separate series, and thus vaulted into the most expensive Chevrolet category available, pushing the Impala into the second most expensive position. In 1964, Chevrolet sold Super Sports only as two-door Sport Coupes, four-door Sport Sedans, and convertibles.

Showroom Hemi V8 versions didn't arrive until 1965, but MOPAR already had its equally high horsepower B and RB 'Wedge' V8s, with the Max Wedge pumping out 425hp!

The horsepower war was well under way, and the Impala and Impala SS were right in the middle of it. With engines nearing the maximum in power and cubic inches, in 1965 Chevrolet was set to counter attack with all-new styling and chassis refinement to maintain its status.

The four-door hardtop or Sport Sedan Impala was always stunning in looks while providing increased practicality in passenger transport. The refined styling of the 1964 models featured a stately, sophisticated sculptured grille. Upmarket Impala options included power steering, power brakes, power windows, and a six-way power 'Flexomatic' front seat. Other available additions included a deluxe AM/FM push-button radio, a 'Comfortilt' steering wheel, Four Season air-conditioning, and tinted glass.

Opposite: The '64 Impala Station Wagon seen here in Palomar Red remained unchanged in regards to size, specifications, and model availability. Popular station wagon options included a luggage roof rack and a split second seat, with a choice of a one-third or two-thirds fold-down section to conveniently accommodate a variety of loads and passenger numbers.

1964 once again saw a full range of the Impala models, which included the Sport Coupe, convertible, four-door sedan and Sport Sedan, and station wagon. The Impala Sport Coupe or Sport Coupe SS could be ordered with a contrasting white or black vinyl roof as an optional extra.

Impala Sport Coupe in Lagoon Aqua

Impala 4-Door Sedan in Palomar Red

STATION WAGONS

Even awkward angles and a skewed perspective couldn't detract from the chic disposition of the '64 Impala Convertible. The price of a new Impala Convertible started at $3035US. For the added SS trim, buyers would have to ante up an additional $175US. Chevrolet produced 81,897 Impala Convertibles in 1964, and it has been estimated that six to ten per cent of the 185,325 Super Sports ordered were ragtops. Perhaps the Impala wasn't as distinctive as it once was, but the convertible was still a head-turner.

Performance, style, and statement: a dream car for all ages – 1965-1966

By 1965 the full-size Chevrolet lines accounted for over 33 per cent of GM's total sales and 60 per cent of that 33 per cent were Impala buyers.

For 1965 Chevrolet had thrown out all the previous looks despite the full-size Chevy's success. Gone was last the boxy, squared-off look, replaced with a smoother, rounder style, but with sharp fender creases and numerous styling cues borrowed from Chevrolet's rubber-burning, race-successful, image-loaded, Corvette Sting Ray.

Motor Trend magazine in its *'65 Auto Show Issue* (11/64) loved the styling stating, "... the Impala's secret is that it does have a lively and individual design flair – more than ever." The styling analysis went on to state the overall shape provided, "... a foundation of intentional definition that justifies the youthful, smooth statement to everyone."

Chassis-wise, the new full-size Chevrolets were radically changed, sitting on a new wide-track perimeter frame (2in in front, 3in in rear), with a redesigned front and rear suspension. These changes improved the handling, ride and comfort.

Another area of improvement noted in a *Motor Trend* (12/64) test was the resolution to the longtime problem of the awkward steering wheel angle and driving position, which had been a continual criticism of the Impala since 1958.

The Impala was a recognized performance car in 1965, and many manufacturers were more than happy to brag about the fact they had something to do with it. The Champion Spark Plug Company of Toledo, Ohio noted in its national advertising that 49 out of 50 Chevrolets accelerated faster with Champion spark plugs installed. The Impala four-door hardtop was pictured. The 1965 Impala was heavier (3475lb), 2in longer (213in), and 2in wider (79.6in).

The 1965 restyled Chevrolet Impala convertible was improved in many small but convenient ways. The rear window

in the convertible top was no longer plastic, but rather, no-worry tempered glass. Also new were safer, fork-like door latches; an easier to open pop-up hood release; and less rattling and scuttle shake, thanks to added body mounts. When powered by the standard, 283ci V8, it sold for $2988US. The Impala trunk was easy to load with its low lip and 19ft³ capacity. Sales slumped from 1964's total of 889,600 Impalas to 803,400, but those included the new Caprice option. A total of 243,114 were SS coupe and convertible models. (Courtesy Country Classic Cars)

The newest Impala was super smooth on turnpikes, less so on rough roads, but overall designed to fit every American's dream. Yet, although a reliable, comfortable, nicely appointed, well-designed, stylish automobile, with ample power, the Impala *Motor Trend* road test conveyed little real enthusiasm.

Car & Driver (12/64) tested a "considerably civilized" 340hp, 409ci Impala SS, and stated that "In present trim, the Chevrolet Impala is a large, silent automobile, more closely related to the Oldsmobile Dynamic 88 and Pontiac Catalina than any of the smaller cars in the General Motors scheme of things ... the Impala has shed all pretensions of trying to look like a chromed-up economy car and is coming on like a full-fledged member of the medium-priced field."

In 1965 Chevrolet also introduced a 'Caprice'

Irresistible force – in an irresistible object '65 CHEVROLET 409

The Chevrolet 409 was relatively short-lived as the biggest V8, but had become legendary and continued to be an option for the production line '65 Impala. It could be ordered in two forms. There was the 340hp, 4bbl with hydraulic lifters, and a 10.0:1 compression ratio, or as a 400hp, 4bbl, with mechanical lifters and an 11.0:1 compression ratio. The 409 was no longer king of the road, but the rumoured smoother 396ci V8 replacement would supplement it midway in '65. The 396ci V8 was a direct derivative of the Daytona/NASCAR Chevrolet 425ci 'porcupine-head' and would be pumping-out 325hp.

option. For a mere $200US you could morph your Impala four-door hardtop Sport Sedan into a luxurious and visually distinctive Impala. A black grille, vinyl roof, different sill trim, badges, and wheel covers were only part of the package. As well as being immediately recognizable, the more exclusive Caprice rode on a stiffer frame and overall upgraded suspension.

This new Impala was a far cry from the car of the American Gran Turismo crowd it attracted in 1958. The market and times had changed by 1965, and the Impala along with it; more changes were coming.

In 1966, just as the Impala had evolved into a separate series, the new top-of-the-line Caprice series was now offered in two-door, four-door, hardtop, and station wagon models, all with V8 power only.

The introduction of the new Caprice, the

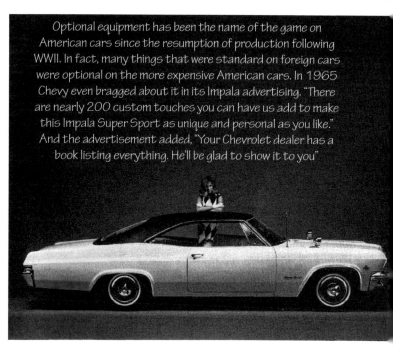

A special Chevrolet we'll practically custom tailor for you

Impala convertible brochure shots continued to feature fashionable, and obviously successful young women. The Impala dream and image maker was no longer male dominated. The women's liberation movement was rightfully gaining momentum, and more and more women were buying the automobile of their choice and not their husband's. Both the Sport Coupe and convertible were offered with a 'Sports Option.' The 1966 Impala Convertible retailed for $3041US, while the open SS version sold for $3199US.

nationwide hoopla surrounding Ford's Mustang, the ever increasing popularity of the Chevy Chevelle – which, in addition, featured all-new styling and options in 1966 – combined with the watering down of the original Impala concept led to a dramatic dip in sales.

Another factor in the decline was the very mild face-lift appearance of the '66 Impala and the hope the '67 version would incorporate the styling cues seen on the Concours show car unveiled at New York Auto Show.

Still, all was not lost as Chevrolet introduced a

CAR LIFE

1966 AT FORD
MERCURY
DODGE
PLYMOUTH
CHRYSLER

{ Chevrolets
Are Back
In Racing!

potent 390hp or 425hp, 427ci engine that garnered lots of press, if not sales. Yet, over a decade later automotive journalists would look back at the 1965-66 Chevrolet Impala line-up and declare that it was – in all probability – the best American car ever built. It was the epitome of American design, style, reliability, and comfort in a USA-built automobile. Alas, like most good things in life, it wasn't fully appreciated in its day.

The biggest news on the full-size Chevy front in 1966 was the addition of the 427ci V8. An enlarged 396, the 427ci V8 became the overnight darling of stoplight street racers, as well as the publicity rich stock car and dragster events. When combined with the (also optional) 327ci and 396ci, these three V8s provided Chevrolet with one, two, and pow – the knockout punch!

The 1966 Impala interior was perhaps not as luxurious as the Caprice's, but it was a considerable upgrade from the Bel Air and base model Biscayne station wagons. Standard fittings included deep-twist nylon carpeting and a full range of six matching colors, such as the blue seen here. The interior was covered in the current popular and highly durable vinyl materials, and even the seatbelts were color-keyed. Other standard features included padded sun visors, back-up and glove box lights, an electric clock, power tailgate glass on the three-seat wagons, and dual speed windscreen wipers. A new option was the telescopic tilt steering wheel.

This 1966 Impala SS Sport Coupe model in Regal Red was one of 199,300 built (including convertibles). The Sport Coupe featured bucket seats as standard equipment, and included on the convertible with the Sports Option. Out of that total 116,400 were V8-powered, while, strangely enough, 900 were sold as six-cylinder models. The Sport Coupe with its very 'sporty' roof design had a base price of $2798US, while the SS model prices started at $2947US. Interestingly, the majority sold for over $3500US when optioned with bigger V8s, upgraded radios, air-conditioning and a host of other extras.

In 1966, the signature Impala dual cluster of three separate round taillights surrendered to a less expensive wrap-around, three-cluster, rectangular unit to suggest the traditional styling cue. The highly practical, 3565lb Impala family four-door sedan had a base sticker price of $2783US. Most sedan buyers added the new, optional Turbo Hydra-Matic automatic transmission. This sedan was painted in the more subdued Aztec Brown Metallic, and also sports the optional stainless wheel opening trim, full-wheel discs, and narrow whitewall tires.

Whereas base Chevy '66 station wagons were 'family haulers,' the upmarket Impalas emanated an air of exclusivity, and were right at home at the yacht club or business luncheons, yet they also possessed some sporty pretensions. Like all Impalas, the station wagon featured the new full-length body side moldings. For 1966 your Impala was offered in 15 different exterior colors (Marina Blue pictured), of which six were new, plus eight more two-tone combinations. When the Impala wagon was ordered with two rows of seats it came equipped with an opening rear window that depended on an outside crank-operated handle. Both Impala wagons featured folding flat seats and a counterbalanced, fold-down tailgate.

The 1966 Chevrolet Impala line-up included a handsome and sophisticated four-door station wagon. There was no visual exterior difference between the two-seat wagons and the three-seat models. Both were 213.2in long and built on

the same 119in wheelbase. Total Impala production plummeted to 654,900, of which 621,800 were V8-powered, while a mere 33,100 were six-cylinder cars. A total of 18,100 in the full-size Chevrolet station wagon line-up (including Impalas) were powered by the six-cylinder engine, but the V8-powered examples far exceeded that total at 167,400 station wagons. The two-seat station wagon pictured was painted Lemonwood Yellow in the factory.

1967–1970 and the fading of the American dream ...

This Aqua-colored 1967 Chevrolet Impala convertible was powered by the popular, and more than adequately potent, 275hp, 327ci V8. The steel wheels were enhanced by a set of narrow whitewall tires; optional upgrades included wire wheel discs.

A fresh body design was introduced in 1967, however, it was dimensionally and externally very similar to its predecessors, resulting in the new Impala styling being more evolutionary than revolutionary. A sweeping roofline was unique to the high style 1967 Chevrolet Sport Coupe models, which sold for a base price of $2845US. There was no Impala two-door sedan or formal roofline coupe in the model line-up. Externally, the Sport Coupe differed from the Super Sport models in trim, with the SS cars having less chrome and trim, but fitted with a highly fashionable blacked-out grille.

As well as lacking the prized SS emblems, the lesser, sweptback Impala Sport Coupes sported narrow chrome rocker trim and mid-section body trim, but did not have wheelarch fender trim. Both Sport Coupe models were built on the same 119in wheelbase, and had the overall length of 213.2in.

At a glance, many Impala buyers thought the 1967 models had only been face-lifted, when in reality, the full-size Chevrolets sported all-new sheet metal.

Mechanically little had changed, and the Impala SS could still be ordered with the rather anemic 155hp six.

Motor Trend (3/7) performed a back-to-back-to-back road test on the three dominant leaders in the full-size field, comparing the 1967 Galaxie 500, the Plymouth Sport Fury, and the Chevrolet Impala Super Sport.

Whereas the 1958 Impala was built for the individual, and was very unique, the three 1967 competitors "... revealed the sameness of Detroit products more than it did differences."

A closer look at the three uncovered the fact that all three had the same 119in wheelbase; all were within an inch of being the same length and within a

Special markings.   Special suspension standard.   You can add 4 on the floor . . .   or disc brakes up front.   Mark of Excellence.

Chevrolet gives you that sure feeling

CHEVROLET

"Super" was certainly the word for the 1967 Impala SS 427. It was unabashedly described in Chevy advertisement as, "… a swashbuckling new species of Chevrolet." The bulging hood screamed 385hp or 425hp, 427 down there. Redline tires were popular as a sporty performance aggrandizement, as was four-on-the-floor shifting. Surprisingly, the floor gearshift was an optional extra, as were the highly recommended front disc brakes.

A major factor in Chevrolet's continual growth as a GM Division was its ability to design and build reliable automobiles. Yet, in 1967, Chevrolet widely advertised the fact in motoring publications that it offered lots of added accessories as well as an extensive five-year or 50,000 mile warranty applied to every six-cylinder and V8 engine it built "including both our 396s and all four of our 427s."

100lb in weight; all powered by 315-325hp, 383ci to 396ci V8 engines; and the trio were all capable of 0-60 acceleration times of just over 9 seconds.

All three bore the same exterior styling cues – long hood, shorter deck, Coke bottle sweep to the rear fenders, a sloping roofline, and a lack of side trim that made them all susceptible to parking lot dings and chips.

Vinyl interiors and fitted nylon carpeting throughout were standard, as were the 15in steel wheels.

Ford, Plymouth, and Chevrolet priced their cars competitively; the standard features were virtually carbon copied, and they were optioned similarly.

Really, none had serious vices, although the competitors in this market did differ somewhat in general quality of fit and finish, the number of rattles, and in overall quietness. And, in resale value, the Chevy Impala topped them all.

During testing, the Impala scored high in driver comfort, visibility, dashboard layout, interior and instrument ergonomics, and overall accommodation.

The styling of the 1967 Impala was composed of smooth flanks with a mixture of long creases and some subtle curves. There was a hint of Coke bottle styling, while the added lower fender skirts provided a lean, uncluttered look. The Chevrolet Impala convertible weighed in at a hefty 3625lb. (Courtesy Country Classic Cars)

In the area of handling and roadability though, the Impala fell short.

Motor Trend stated, "We can't foresee the Super Sport Impala ever being awarded top honours in a parking lot slalom ..." Still, the road testers had to confess the handling was far from unpredictable or dangerous, and the Impala did have the best brakes of the bunch.

They concluded, "Chevrolet has come up the quality control list quite a ways, but still has a way to go. The Super Sport's road-worthiness is a compromise between sporty car cornering and luxury car cruising, with emphasis on the latter."

In 1968, Chevrolet Impala sales would rebound upward despite just the mild revamp in styling. As well as reworked front and rear end designs, the fastback hardtop roofline got an even faster look.

The upscale Caprice came standard with hide-away headlights, and this was soon an available option on the Impala. Hide-away wipers were standard on all full-size Chevrolets, yet it was a feature that would be abandoned as, although it cleaned-up the cowl area, those in snowy and icy climates were quick to complain when the wipers were frozen in place, or the wiper motors burned out.

The standard V8 was no longer the reliable 283ci engine. It was replaced in 1968 by an enlarged 307ci V8 via a change in bore and stroke. Most found the 200hp, 307ci V8 a little anemic and opted for the standard 250hp, 327ci V8. (Not surprisingly, today the 307ci V8 is not popular with enthusiasts.)

Other changes in specifications included an improvement in body mounts, hence an improvement in both quietness and ride quality. The perimeter frame was stiffened and new rear and transmission crossmembers were added.

Additional safety measures were regulated in 1968

A total of 556,800 V8 Impalas were sold in 1967 compared to just 18,800 fitted with the six cylinder. Super Sport production was an impressive 76,005, but only 2124 were equipped with the all-powerful 385hp, 427ci V8, and, surprisingly, 400 were sold with the 250ci six-cylinder.

Opposite: This 1967 Impala Model 16467 was Chevrolet's low price convertible at $3097US, while the Impala Super Sport convertible Model 16867 was the Division's most expensive with a base price of $3254US. This particular example was outfitted with the 327ci V8 and the three-speed automatic transmission, whitewall tires, wheel discs, power brakes and power steering, a radio, and deluxe seatbelts.

The Deluxe seatbelts were color-keyed to the interior. The 1967 Impala Deluxe steering wheel featured chrome trim and hub, plus horn buttons built into the spokes of the wheel. This safety feature allowed the driver to 'honk' at friends or other motorists just using their thumbs, and thus without removing their hands.

Opposite: The 1967 Impala series was fitted with two sets of three rear lights, but the middle ones were backup units. Set again in a cluster, the rear lights sat above the back bumper. For the second year in a row the full-size Chevrolet was lower. It was the first year for the hot Mustang versus the new Chevrolet Camaro. This pair competed for the younger potential Impala buyers. Those younger buyers, not requiring such a big ride, were easily attracted to Chevrolet's new 'pony car.' Yet, Impala sales increased slightly.

as were new pollution standards. Performance would soon be dramatically affected in the upcoming years.

Changes in the line-up in '68 included the Super Sport no longer returning as a separate series. As a result, sales suffered and only 38,210 chose the $179US SS option for their Sport Coupe, convertible, or new, Caprice-like Custom Coupe.

A mere 1788 enthusiasts opted for the SS 427ci V8 RPO Z03 that, in itself, had certain power choices: for an extra $358US, 4071 buyers ordered the SS 385hp,

For 1968 Chevrolet freshened its full-size Chevrolet line-up. The most noticeable and controversial change was the implanting of the sets of three (once again) rear taillights in the back bumper. Although it was stylish, and in some ways practical, it was totally unrealistic as far as insurance companies and daily crowded city parking lot users were concerned. The lower level caused problems in heavy traffic, as did snow accumulation in northern climates.

As always, the rear seat of an Impala provided plenty of room for three adults, although the drivetrain hump through the center meant riding with knees high, or legs straddled. This 1968 two-door wasn't as spacious in regards to head, foot or legroom. The rear seating area remains original factory-installed to this day.

427ci V8 RPO Z24, L36 Turbo-Jet package. By adding yet another $525US, 568 enthusiasts went all out for the SS 425hp, 427ci V8 RPO Z24, L72 Turbo-Jet package.

For 1968, the full-size Chevrolets were offered in four series, with 18 different models.

Motor Trend (11/67) retested an Impala SS 427 and summarized with, "A two-year lapse had occurred since

One of the less commonly seen 1968 Impala models was the Custom Coupe or hardtop, Model 16447. Most were sold with the increasingly popular vinyl roof treatment. The vinyl roof would soon become as common on four-door sedans, but in the latter half of the 1960s it was more to provide a formal, 'dressy' look or a sportier, convertible-like appearance without the threat of leaks. First seen on the new top-of-the-line Caprice models, it was offered (sans the vinyl roof) on the Impala in 1968 at a base price of $3021US. A choice of different side trim was offered.

we last drove one. We were amazed at the progress in handling and agility that had been made. Steering response and manners were equal to what we expected from a smaller, lighter car."

Once again, the Impala name appeared to be gold with buyers, as it provided everything most American consumers wanted in an automobile – style, comfort, performance, and rugged reliability.

As the decade wound down, Chevrolet, Ford and Chrysler-Plymouth/Dodge, all restyled their full-size line-ups. While the Big Three did well selling their sporty 'Pony Cars,' compacts, intermediates, and trucks, their bread-and-butter volume cars were their full-size models.

Ford had closed the highest sales/production gap, and was selling just 100,000 cars less a year than the perennial leader Chevrolet. (Ford had not made a serious challenge to Chevrolet's domination of the market since 1959!)

Apart from Chevrolet retaining its four series:

(continues on page 65)

Above: The 1968 Impala two-door hardtop was a handsome, subtle design, with flowing lines and a rakish, stylish roofline. The added chrome drip rails, wheel well, and rocker trim were unique to the Impala. With its full range of big V8s it was a bit of a 'Q-ship' that could be driven on weekdays for conservative business uses, but also with real gusto on weekends – on the road, or possibly on the track with some modifications. The non-original wheels and hubcaps mounted on this example were offered on later models.

The Chevrolet Impala four-door hardtop was still seen as a stylish, trend-setting automobile in 1968. Here, aluminum supplier Alcoa pushes 'beauty' on three levels at one time. The advertisement concluded with the rather sexist line, "As the lovely young model said, 'Aluminum trim can outshine any star! Well, almost, any star,' she added, with a flutter of her eyelashes."

Opposite: In 1968 the Impala was the top selling model in the full-size Chevrolet line. As well as the two-door fastback hardtop, a more formal, originally Caprice exclusive, coach-like 'Custom Hardtop' was added. Other Impala models offered included a four-door sedan and hardtop, and a station wagon (which cost more than the exclusive convertible). In total, approximately 710,900 Impalas were built in 1968. The SS, or Super Sport, once again became an optional equipment package rather than a designated series model.

Change for the better with Alcoa Aluminum

◈ALCOA

While the level of luxury in 1968 can appear to be Spartan in today's world, the Impala was considered well-appointed and high end for a Chevrolet compared to lesser models in its size and price range. This Impala is all original (other than a slightly later AM/FM/cassette radio). Note the Deluxe steering wheel, and the polished aluminum trim on the seat, which had been a longtime added Impala feature.

Regardless of the Impala year or bodystyle it always had an enormous trunk for hauling a family's groceries, luggage for vacations, or most anything else. The placement of the spare tire was not optimal, but, as the years slipped by, both the roads and tires improved considerably which greatly reduced the chances of a flat. Note original bias ply spare tire. The basic Chevrolet Biscayne model hubcap was added as a bit of dressing-up because the usual cut-to-fit, grey and black, vinyl trunk floor mat was missing.

The 200bhp, 307ci V8 was a popular middle-of-the-road engine choice in 1968. This smaller engine provided more than adequate power on the highway, while delivering better gas mileage. Note the now-typical aftermarket, non-original Chevrolet polished air breather and valve covers, and a chromed dual brake master cylinder cap.

Performance was selling cars in 1969, and Chevrolet as a Division was facing tough competition not only from Ford and Chrysler, but also from within GM itself. Pontiac, Buick, and Oldsmobile all had sporty, high-performance models. Chevrolet had the biggest line-up of performance cars from GM, which included its compact Nova SS, pony car Camaro SS, Corvette sports car, intermediate Chevelle SS, as well as its full-size Impala 427 SS. Thus, while the Impala had to also compete within the Chevrolet Division itself, there was also a growing trend toward smaller cars.

Biscayne, Bel Air, Impala, and Caprice; its four-coil spring suspension; and 119in wheelbase; everything else was new, replaced, or reconfigured for 1969.

The new bodies were 215.9in long – the longest ever! (GM was still a strong proponent of 'Bigger is Better,' and it was also possible to option-out a Caprice to the point that it was costlier than a new full-size, basic Cadillac.)

While the two lowest Chevrolet Series, Biscayne and Bel Air, were only offered in lowly two and four-door sedans, the Impala offered the full range of models (except a two-door post sedan).

The Caprice was available only as a two-door

and four-door hardtop, and the station wagons were sold at Caprice and Impala trim levels, but bearing the nameplate Kingswood Estate and Kingswood respectively.

All GM cars, including the Impalas, were built with side impact barriers through the use of steel beams built into each door, along with reinforcements added to the body pillars. The barriers were designed to reduce interior penetration in collisions, and would soon be mandated by Federal regulations.

From a styling viewpoint, the press tended to praise the Impala's new, subtly different looks. Its front bumper and grille were fully integrated into the body, as was its

(continues on page 68)

Opposite: Despite the fact that smaller and lighter model '69 Chevys in the Division could be ordered with the same rubber burning V8s, the better appointed Impala SS 427 was the far more sophisticated and 'mature' muscle car with prestige. The high powered V8 Chevelle and Nova with lower base sticker prices required a long list of optional equipment to approach the standards on the Impala equivalent. (Note the older Impala owner couple – although far younger than couples pictured in Caprice ads and brochures. As well, the models are African American, which would have been sadly unheard of in a brochure just a few years before.) (Canadian brochure)

IMPALA

Opposite: For 1969 Chevrolet again offered its – almost identical to the top-of-the-line Caprice – Impala Custom Coupe with the same formal roofline. The specifications were virtually the same, although there was fractionally more overall room inside the Impala. (This was due to marginally less padding and different panel and seating materials.) The base 335hp, 427ci V8 could be ordered on both, but the lowly 250ci six-cylinder engine could only be ordered for the Impala. However, the Caprice was only offered as a two-door and four-door hardtop, with that formal roofline that conveyed luxury rather than sportiness or performance, which were still the Impala's domain.

The Impala Sport Coupe pictured here had the unique sweeping roofline, but it was the Custom Coupe that was described as having a 'custom roof,' which featured a concave rear window. The SS 427 came only in Sport Coupe and convertible models, and featured a black accented front grille, 15in wheels and lots of SS emblems. That was all pretty subtle, except for the whopping 390hp, 427 V8 under the hood! The lock and load Impala SS was ready, yet it would be the last year for the SS models, despite the fact that nearly a million had been ordered since 1961.

rear bumper, which continued to house the twin triple bank of taillights. The taillights were rectangular in shape to provide a fresher look.

The Coke bottle shaped rear fender was there, and, apart from a lower belt line and around the wheel wells, the styling was smooth and uncluttered. Most applauded were the swelled, flared-like bulges on each wheel well, but some likened them to a young man's cheek full of chewing tobacco. Yup!

Front vent windows were no longer offered, much to the chagrin of many. While lazy cigarette smokers had loved them for flicking ash, the majority of buyers found them a noisy way of providing cool air into the passenger compartment. Yet, it was a moot point with the ever-increasing popularity of air-conditioning.

The non-enthusiast, but popular buyer's magazine *Consumer Reports* (1/69), tested five popular full-size cars: the Ford Galaxie 500, Pontiac Catalina, AMC Ambassador DPL, Plymouth Fury III, and the Chevrolet Impala.

Although the road test concluded the five makes were greatly alike, there were significant differences.

An annual comparison, *Consumer Reports* rated the Ford Galaxie 500 best overall for the second year in a row. The Impala 235hp, 327ci V8, four-door sedan was rated second best.

Surveys were used by *Consumer Reports* to determine reliability, and, like all surveys, the results did not always reflect the feelings of all owners. Regardless, the findings were always an indication of a cross-section of buyers' experiences.

In the 1969 Impala testing, *Consumer Reports* stressed, "... a competent performer in nearly all respects, remember it behaves like its predecessors ... over the years it will spend more time than the others in the shop for repairs. On the other hand, the 1969 Impala has a good many truly new parts and components; perhaps they'll prove more reliable than the old."

Motor Trend (11/69) published a four car company

The Impala vinyl interiors reflected the youthful, sporty nature of the car, while hinting at luxury well above the sober-looking Bel Air and Biscayne. The brocades were left to the Caprice models. In 1969 the base price for a Caprice Custom Coupe was $3277US, while the same style Impala cost $3068US. The Impala also came in a sportier two-door hardtop with a more sweeping roof treatment at $3016US. The extensively restyled big Chevrolet retained its 119in wheelbase, but added length to a stretched 215.9in.

The Impala was offered in two-door Custom Coupe, Sport Coupe, convertible, four-door hardtop, and sedan. Chevrolet, under the guidance of John DeLorean, built 1,109,013 full-size Chevrolets in 1969, of which 777,000 were Impalas, although that also included the Kingswood station wagons that were sold with Impala level equipment. Yet, out of that, a mere 14,415 were convertibles, and, surprisingly, only 2425 ragtop Impalas were purchased with the SS option. Impala buyers, for the most part, were putting luxury and adequate power – only 8700 buyers chose the six-cylinder engine – before all-out muscle car performance. The times, once again, were a-changing.

comparison test, albeit the Chevrolet compared was a 427ci V8 prototype that it had tested earlier in July at the GM proving grounds. (Having personally driven prototypes of pre-production models, this was not always representative of the model that arrived on the showroom floor.)

Nevertheless, comparing the sportier '69 Ford LTD, Plymouth Fury III, AMC Ambassador SST, and Chevrolet Impala two-door hardtops, *Motor Trend* concluded that the bottoming-out of the suspension on rough roads, the seating position, and lack of rear seat room were the Impala's most objectionable deficiencies, while the "... ride and handling are primary among plus features." Praise was also bestowed on the comfortable front bucket seats, the huge trunk, and the Impala's styling being "... bon vivant among the big car set."

There were changes in the Chevrolet full-size

line-up in 1970. The longstanding Biscayne and Bel Air models were down to just a four-door sedan and differed only in trim.

The model line-ups remained the same on the Impala and Caprice, but the Caprice was no longer the prestige Chevrolet, having relinquished that crown to the new, one model only Monte Carlo two-door hardtop.

There was a new 155hp, 250ci six, but all Impala and Caprice models were powered by V8s. Of the many optional V8s, the 345hp or 390hp, 454ci was the largest V8 offered by Chevrolet. It replaced the 427ci V8 in some the Chevy line-ups.

Size was still important, and Chevy sold 22,585 of these monster 454ci V8s in its Impala, Corvette, Chevelle, and truck lines.

The 327ci V8 was dropped in favor of the more powerful 350ci V8. This was mostly to offset the increase

Left: Chevrolet still promoted its 1970 Impala to the younger crowd, but, by the end of the decade, younger couples and college kids were hot for a sportier Camaro or an intermediate-sized Chevelle. As well, the Impala had now been eclipsed by an additional model within the Division itself. The all-new Monte Carlo was now seen as Chevrolet's main competition for the Thunderbird. Although well dressed, the Impala had evolved slowly into the mainstream, bread-and-butter Chevy model. Few buyers wanted a lowly basic Biscayne or slightly upmarket Bel Air. Model year production of full-size Chevrolets fell to 550,571 with the bulk being the Impala series.

in popularity of the power-draining options such as air-conditioning.

As a Division, Chevrolet still offered 302ci, 307ci, 396ci, 400ci, and 402ci V8s, plus a smaller six and a four-cylinder engine. The base V8 offered in the Impala was a 250hp, 350ci, but a more powerful 350 V8 was also available.

Having undergone extensive changes in 1969, the new Impala was subjected to only minor styling changes in 1970. Gone was the wrap-around bumper in favour of an angular, contour-fitted, slim bumper cutting through the lower third of a large checkerboard grille. The two clusters of three rectangular taillights were now predominantly vertical rather than horizontal. The restyled wheel discs for 1970 were considered very unattractive by many.

Consumer Reports (2/70) repeated its annual same model, full-size, five-car road test, this time featuring cars with over 400ci V8s (except the 390ci AMC Ambassador).

The 454ci V8 Impala was praised for smoothness, but criticized as sluggish at city traffic speeds. The magazine's findings were virtually identical with the previous year. Once again the Impala was second best with its reliability and frequency of repair still seen as a negative. *Consumer Reports* felt the new 265hp, 400ci

Opposite: In 1970, Chevrolet offered Impala buyers a choice of three different interiors. A cloth and vinyl interior was standard on all Impala models except the convertible which sported a more practical, all vinyl interior. The wide range of colors available included medium blue, gold, dark green, turquoise, and black. You could order the all vinyl interior on your coupe or sedan in saddle, medium gold, medium blue, dark green, sandalwood, red, or black. The convertible vinyl interior was obtainable in black, green, red, or saddle.

V8 (formerly the 396) was the best engine to select, and the heavy-duty suspension not worth ordering unless buyers opted for the 454ci V8.

Certainly these cars were comfortable, but, most of the time, the one or two people in the car didn't require all that interior space: substantially more overall interior space did not necessarily equal greater creature comfort for just two passengers.

When comparison testing, *Motor Trend* (3/70) found that the 1970 Dodge Polara, AMC Ambassador, Ford XL, and Chevrolet Impala all performed well and accomplished the goals set out.

"Each of the cars shines more predominantly in some areas, but in the total relationship of ride, comfort, handling, performance and convenience, the Impala 350 has the edge."

Other changes were now taking place in America. Although fuel was inexpensive in North America in 1970, the mileage figures for a new Impala – although better than in 1958 – tended to range from just 8mpg in the city to a high of a mere 14mpg on the highway. (A 1970 Sunbeam Arrow four-door sedan returned a figure closer to 25mpg or more.)

Yet, while the cost of fuel was a factor, the cost of car insurance in North America in 1970 was escalating at an unbelievable rate.

In 1970, a male driver under 21-years of age with one accident, or even speeding ticket, was paying an annual insurance premium of around $2200US if he purchased a $4000US performance car.

By 1970, the press was becoming more and more vocal about the overall bulk of the American full-size model cars. Yet, in 1971, Chevrolet appeared to be deaf to such criticism, and introduced an all-new, even larger Impala. The overall length grew slightly by 0.8in to 216.8in, while

Changes to the 1970 full-size Chevy line amounted to a reconfigured front fender line, hood, and grille, and a minor restyling to the rear end. The standard V8 was the 250hp, 350ci motor, with the much-loved 327ci no longer offered. (Chevrolet enthusiasts would soon embrace the Chevy 350ci V8, and it was well on its way to becoming the ultimate American V8 of rebuilders, hot rodders, and custom car enthusiasts.)

the wheelbase jumped from 119in to 121.5in.

That increase in itself was somewhat significant from a Division that was pushing its tiny Vega, four-cylinder economy car, but even more so when compared to the original 1958 Impala with its overall length of just 209in and a wheelbase of 117.5in. The 1971 Chevrolet was even bigger than the luxury liner 1958 Cadillac.

Most importantly, when introduced in 1958 the Chevrolet Impala was a very special, prestigious and unique model, but, by 1971, it was Chevrolet Division's money maker. The tiny, inexpensive Vega had an equally tiny profit margin. Even when 400,000 examples might be delivered, or all the options were ordered by a customer – which was seldom – the high volume profit just wasn't there.

Pushing high production had drained the Impala of

all its character. Even an arm long option list couldn't individualize the Impala to the point where anyone was getting too excited.

Car & Driver (10/70) put it this way: "Under close scrutiny, the Impala seems to have grown less by plan than by lack of restraint, like a pot belly that comes with age. And its cautious, evolutionary styling further suggests a car that continues with very little attention to purpose or concept."

The 1971 Impala was nice transportation featuring an all-new chassis, body, and further improvements and upgrades, but in overall engineering and appearance it had changed only slightly and did the same job in relatively the same way.

Meanwhile, the 116in wheelbase, 205in long Monte Carlo was the new head-turner in the large

Officially the trunk featured an 18ft³ capacity, but that includes all the odd shapes and corners. There was also boasting about the Impala's generous interior. The full-size Chevrolets provided ample headroom, shoulder room, hip room (42in), and legroom for six people in the sedans, and five people in the coupes and convertibles. The amount of rear legroom in the latter models was dependent on the size of the front passengers.

While the 1970 Impala was no longer the 'personal car' it once was, it was still an outstanding American car. Power disc brakes were standard on the Impala Custom Coupe – optional on all the other Impala models, full coil suspension, double-acting shock absorbers, ball and race steering, built in levelling for braking and acceleration, a strong perimeter-type frame, and a 14-point body to frame cushioned mounting. Chevrolet stressed minimum maintenance and increased longevity, thanks, in part, to the standard aluminized exhaust system, inner steel fenders, flush and dry rocker panels, self-adjusting brakes, and anti-corrosion brake lines.

You fit in a Big Chevrolet.

Impala 4-Door Sedan

Chevrolet line-up. Built on a Chevelle wheelbase, its long hood, short deck, and formal roof proportions appealed to the American buyer looking for a large, distinctive, stylish, sporty-looking car, but without any in-your-face opulence. It was the new 'personal car' of the 1970s, and substantially less expensive than its competition.

Brock Yates wrote about the Impala in *Car & Driver* (3/71), "Yes, car buffs, despite our denouncements about this dumb, oversized, gross, wasteful, immoral device that is the very namesake, Impala, it remains a reasonable automobile for a substantial segment of the American public."

Any way you looked at it, the Impala was now just reliable, generic transportation, and no longer any American's dream car.

The Impala would soldier on with less horsepower and smaller V8s – and even undergo a down-sizing in 1977 as a reaction to the fear of more gas shortages occurring, fuel prices soaring, and imported cars continuing to grow in popularity.

The 1977 Chevrolet Impala was the *Motor Trend* Car of the Year and continued to sell well, yet ultimately the once-loved nameplate would be abandoned by Chevrolet in 1985.

The Impala SS was reintroduced with great fanfare in 1994, but was devoid of any mystique, and failed to recapture its former glory; it quietly faded from the scene in 1996.

Then again, in 2000, a new front-wheel-drive Impala was introduced, and subsequent generations followed in 2005 and 2013. Current Impala production is scheduled to end in 2020 as a full-size sedan.

At this point, many young people saw the Impala as the car of 'the establishment.' America had become a country in social and racial turmoil with whites against blacks, the hippy generation in opposition to the crew cuts, the youth versus the old establishment, and the 'Hawks' as opposed to the 'Doves' over Vietnam. The Impala had slowly been watered down to become every American's car rather than a 'personal car.' And, with the sales of smaller, imported cars rocketing upward, the big Impala was starting to look more like a dinosaur.

Custom Impalas

The meaning of the term 'customizing' bears little resemblance to those early days in the 1950s when the legendary likes of George and Sam Barris, Gene Winfield, Bill Cushenbury, and others developed the look by chopping, channelling, frenching, lowering, etc, bodies, modifying all the mechanicals, and taking automotive paintwork from a basic coating of the metal to colorful rolling artworks.

As the decades slipped by and we entered the new millennium, the original 'custom' definition spread like butter to include any modified postwar car.

Enthusiasts attempted to develop niche meanings under the custom car umbrella with the addition of Rat Rods, Resto Rods, Resto Mods, Street Machines, and other assorted terms.

Today, virtually all makes and models have been embraced by the hands of customizers who desire to evolve the original, factory design team's finished production version, and imbue it with his or her own vision of restyling and beautification.

With customizing being such a personal statement, it is not surprising to discover that the Chevrolet Impala models built from 1958 to 1970 are the perfect base due to its inherent all-American style, trim level, solid performance, and overall engineering. It was the Chevrolet personal car, and remains so today in both stock and customized forms.

Sometimes, customizing a vehicle is purely an individual's interpretation, and can range from simple updating of wheels, seats and assorted bits such as stereo systems, handles and chrome treatments, to an all-out complete rebuild in the spirit of the original '50s concepts.

Once seen as just good donor cars for the restoration or customizing of sportier models, station wagons have now become very popular with both camps. From the rear we would envision a mild custom '66 Impala wagon with the popular, weathered-look paint, aftermarket wheels, roof rack with surfboards, vintage state park/vacation window stickers, and a custom interior, but paint and trim effectively stock. Yet, upfront there is a big V8 complete with a chrome blower thrust through the hood ready to howl, "Here's a hot Chevy, waiting to tear-up the road!"

In reality, though, customizing is very often limited by time, money, and/or talent.

With that in mind, and the fact that customizers are unique individuals, they also have certain agendas and parameters in their vision. These range from basic preferences – such as certain colors, wheels, etc – to a full spectrum of modifications incorporating chopping and channeling, to wholesale design changes.

There is also a body of customizers who tend to

focus their artistic endeavors on the power and performance of the car, rather than on cosmetic modifications; these mechanical modifications are, foremost, industrial art.

There are also a small number of automotive customizers whose artistry personifies and embraces their automotive creation with spectacular results. These customizers are, in every nuance of the definition, true artists!

(continues on page 80)

Custom four-door hardtops provide plenty of family room, but can be real '60s cool at the same time. This 1962 bright-red-with-a-black-hardtop Impala has been lowered, fitted with rear fender skirts, and graced with lake pipes for a custom cruisin' look.

This Retro Rod or Transition Wagon, known as the 'Double Bubble,' successfully blends original factory styling cues with a truly unique custom look and upgrade. The 1961 Chevrolet Impala was conceived and executed by Greening Auto Company in Nashville. An additional top from a 1961 Pontiac turned the Impala hardtop into super-stylish hardtop wagon complete with an opening tailgate. The subtle bulge in the hood hints of the powerful 409ci V8 rebuilt to 473ci housed below. (Carol Duckworth, photographer, courtesy Mecum Auctions.)

The same 1961 Impala Retro Rod station wagon was treated to a fully redesigned modern interior, but with a retro look to suit its vintage era. The custom interior creation by Paul Atkins features custom-built, leather, power bucket seats, tilt steering, modern instruments in a hand-built leather dash, custom door panels, carpet, and much more. This super innovative '61 Impala was a 2016 Pirelli Great 8 Finalist. (Carol Duckworth, photographer, courtesy Mecum Auctions.)

The mostly original rear fender styling seamlessly flows into a later period almost Kamm-like tail on this '61 Impala wagon. The door handles, window trim, badging, windshield wipers, moldings, and lettering were removed. The roof pillars were hand-formed, and the roofline was dropped 3in. The front sheet metal was lengthened, and the body joint removed. The Impala was lowered, and the fenders flared to accommodate the extra-wide wheels and tires.
(Carol Duckworth, photographer, courtesy Mecum Auctions.)

Legendary Lowrider Artist and automotive craftsman Albert De Alba painted and worked every external surface of his 1963 Chevrolet Impala in custom candy paint, chrome plating, and metal etching. (Courtesy Petersen Museum & the Elite Car Club)

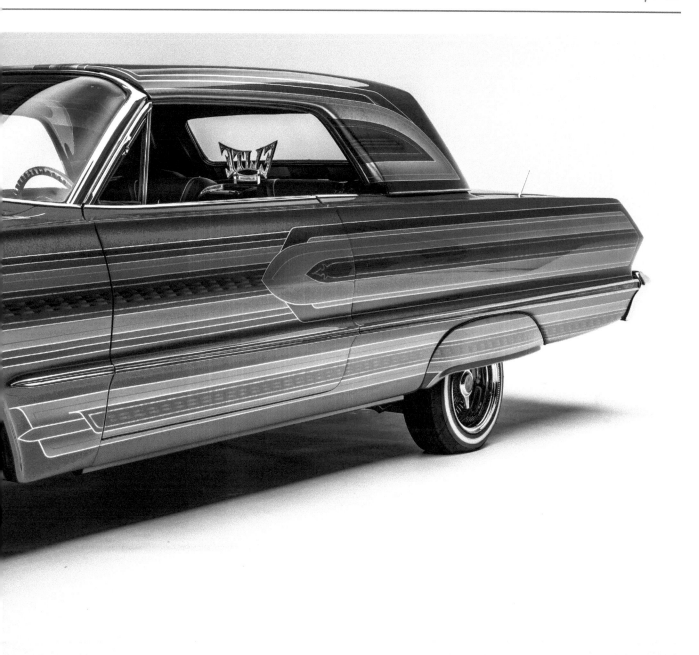

These super talented individuals approach customizing as any other artist would approach a painting or sculpture. Within their artistry they have a totally different interpretation – their life philosophy can influence their work, and cultural symbols can also be seen in the paintwork. The result is an artistic statement or mobile sculpture. Beauty is truly in the eye of the beholder: while some car enthusiasts see the cultural and social implications being conveyed, others just appreciate the artist's work because it's 'cool.'

(continues on page 89)

'El Rey' was created in 2011 by Albert De Alba Sr of Pomona, California. His 1963 Chevrolet Impala lowrider captured top awards and recognition in such respected shows as SEMA and the Grand National Roadster Show in the US. This highly acclaimed Impala was also named 'Lowrider of the Year' by *Lowrider Magazine* for 2011, 2012 and 2013. (Courtesy Petersen Museum & the Elite Car Club)

Through carefully planned and executed geometric paintwork, the Chevrolet Impala's bodylines were accentuated as the images and paint flow over the entire body, into the engine compartment, through the interior, spilling into the trunk, and sweeping over the undercarriage to fully encapsulate its fully functional form. (Courtesy Petersen Museum & the Elite Car Club)

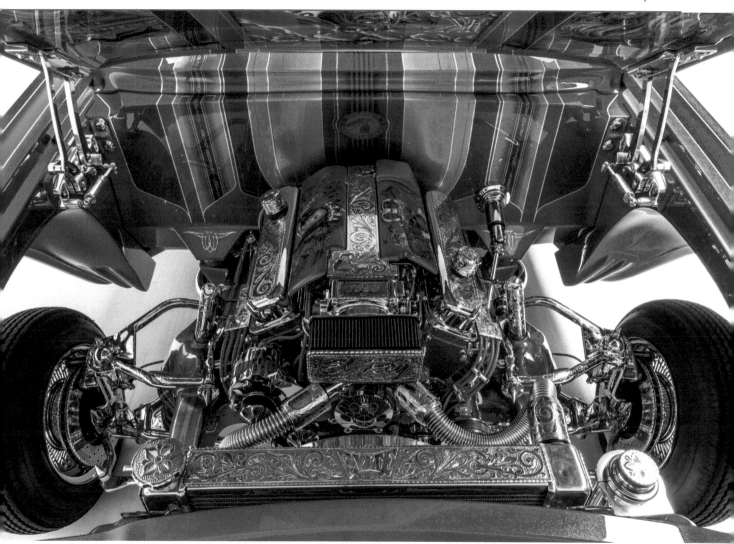

El Rey has been acknowledged as a pinnacle of Lowrider culture, yet it is also regarded as a rolling sculpture in the custom car world. Even the engine went beyond custom detailing to become an elaborate and personal piece of industrial and cultural art. (Courtesy Petersen Museum & the Elite Car Club)

This dramatic 1968 Chevrolet Impala lowrider, dubbed 'El Muertorider,' was built in 2006 by automotive artists Artemio Rodriguez and John Jota Leaños of San Francisco, California. (Courtesy Petersen Museum & the Richard Harris Art Collection)

As well as being a spectacular example of a Chevrolet Impala, Artemio Rodriguez and John Jota Leaños also included a variety of complex themes related to the extensive culture surrounding lowriding. (Courtesy Petersen Museum & the Richard Harris Art Collection)

Opposite: The artwork of John Jota Leaños and Artemio Rodriguez was geared to illustrate aspects of Western art history and Día de los Muertos (Day of the Dead). The theme of the exterior artwork addresses death, war, and policing. The artists noted the radio of the '68 Impala, El Muertorider is tuned to ¡Radio Muerto!, a program created for broadcasting content attempting to decolonize the airwaves and project imagines of a bright future where culture is again allowed to flourish. (Courtesy Petersen Museum & the Richard Harris Art Collection)

With its long national cultural history dating back to 1974, 'Gypsy Rose' is perhaps one of the most recognized lowriders in the world. The 1964 Chevrolet was filmed cruising along Whittier Boulevard in the opening credits of the popular television sitcom, *Chico and the Man*, starring the late comic Freddie Prinze. In 2017, the Gypsy Rose Impala was inducted into the Historic Vehicle Associations National Historic Vehicle Register. (Courtesy Petersen Museum & Jesse Valadez Jr)

A perfect example of this type of automotive artistry or customization has been the subject of numerous exhibits presented by the Petersen Museum in Los Angeles, California.

Lowriders are familiar customs in the United States, and the best of the best have been displayed over the years.

The Petersen Museum has described such exhibits as "The High Art of Riding Low: Ranflas, Corazón e Inspiración." The lowrider car (ranfla) has inspired many artists, but it is especially celebrated by Chicana/o artists throughout the Southwest."

It is widely acknowledged that the lowrider custom cars are symbols of cultural pride (corazón).

These lowriders are icons of everyday life experiences, as well as embodying the formation of multicultural communities through a passion for a specific form of car customization.

A spokesperson for the Petersen Museum noted, "As 'canvases of self-expression,' lowrider customs serve as the basis of artistic creativity (inspiración), inspiring generations of artists to engage with their iconography, performativity, and aesthetics."

More mainstream customizing that can approach this level of creativity and artistry are highly modified Transitions or Resto Rods. These customs combine dedicated restoration with a high level of customizing, hot rodding, and utilization of the latest technology, engines, and suspensions. In some cases, a vintage body is mounted on a brand new chassis powered by a more powerful modern engine and drivetrain.

In many cases today, the best of the Resto Rods and Customs rival or surpass the market values of restored-to-factory specification examples.

The broad appeal of Resto Rods and Customs stems not just from the quality of the build and beautifully executed styling, but also from the practicality of these very unique vehicles by providing modern comfort, safety, performance, and handling.

Thus, while there will always be a market for 'original' Chevrolet Impalas, Resto Rods and Custom Impalas have lots to offer eager enthusiasts, too.

Opposite: The original 1964 Chevrolet Impala-based Gypsy Rose was, sadly, severely damaged in an accident. Due to the car's high regard and cultural importance, Gypsy Rose was fully recreated to original conditions including its 150 hand-painted roses and an interior featuring pink crushed velvet upholstery, chandeliers, and a cocktail bar. It is an important part of the Valadez family heritage and their father's legacy. (Courtesy Petersen Museum & Jesse Valadez Jr)

Overleaf: The famous 1964 Chevrolet Impala is owned by Jesse Valadez Jr who inherited the collection from his father. (Courtesy Petersen Museum & Jesse Valadez Jr)

Jan Karlander's electric-powered 1966 Impala Convertible

Probably the first all-electric Impala in the world, Jan's Impala was electrified in Sweden and was completed in November 2020. Inspected and approved as a converted vehicle by SFRO and then by the Swedish Transport Agency, the car is now tax-exempt, inspection-exempt and fossil-free for the future.

The car uses the entire rear drive unit from a 2015 Tesla model S giving it 550 horsepower. The battery pack is located in the original engine bay in place of the V8 engine and energy storage is 47kWh, giving a range of 200 kilometres (124 miles).

Interesting fact: there are about 6400 Impalas from 1958-1970 in Sweden: that's about one Impala for every 1500 inhabitants. That should be a clue that the Swedes like these cars!

Specification

Driveline: Complete rear drive from Tesla model S, including suspension, drive shafts, brakes and electric parking brake. The Tesla subframe is bolted to the Impala's original frame using four M16 screws, one in each corner.

Battery pack: 18 LG lithium ion battery modules, with approximately 60-volt nominal voltage. Six are connected in series, a so-called string, giving 360 volts and up to 400 volts at full charge. Three strings of six batteries are then connected in parallel, giving up to

Jan in his electric Impala.

2400 amps and 47kWh. The circuit boards on top of the modules are the battery management system (BMS).

Brakes: Disc brakes all round, Tesla at the rear and Wilwood at the front. Two brake master cylinders are connected by a balance bar. There is no servo.

Steering: Electric power steering with adjustable servo action.

Suspension: Air suspension from Ridetech with individual adjustment for each wheel. Shock absorption is also adjustable from soft to hard in 20 steps. New, more modern front control arms from Ridetech.

Wheels: 19x7.5in steel rims with Tesla bolt pattern. Hubcaps are modified 1966 Chevelle, so-called dog dishes.

Headlights: Projector technology and LED lights from Dapper lighting.

Speedometer: Data via GPS. A small box with an electric motor drives a cable that goes to the car's original speedometer. The make is Speedhut. Kits using this system are available in the US too.

The touch screen used to select drive and reverse.

Total weight (without driver): 1940kg

Builders
The car was built by Jan Karlander in Ängelholm with indispensable help from Martin Söderlind in Förslöv and his company, EVES AB. There are videos on YouTube showing the construction process.

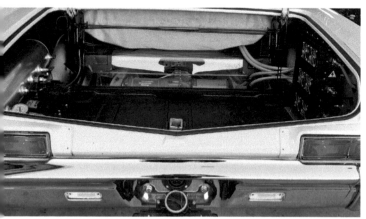

The trunk revealing the drive unit: the on-board charger is on the right and the charging connector at the bottom centre.

No V8 here, just the battery pack with battery management system circuit boards on top.

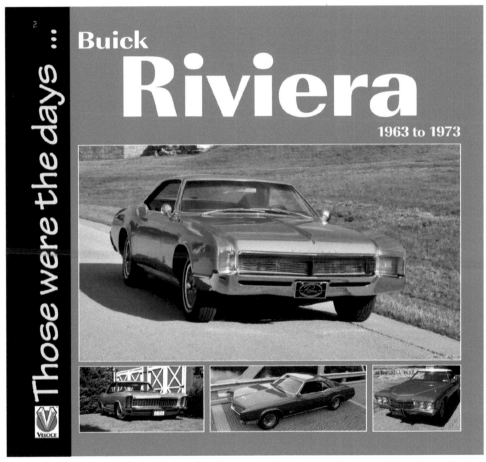

Those were the days ... ™

Buick

Riviera

1963 to 1973

VELOCE

How the Riviera artfully blended styling, luxury, comfort, and performance, from its earliest years as a trim model to its dramatic debut in 1963 as an exciting, unique automobile for the Buick Division. Included are all the pertinent data and information on the 1963 to 1973 Riviera models that enthusiasts will enjoy.

ISBN: 978-1-787113-56-5
Paperback • 19x20.5cm • 96 pages • 110 pictures